Ordinary

By Minda Cox

D0966875

FIELDS PUBLISHING

NASHVILLE, TENNESSEE

Printed in the United States of America
Library of Congress Number 2013955688
ISBN 978-157843-1175

Published by

Fields Publishing, Inc.
8120 Sawyer Brown Road, Suite 108
Nashville, Tennessee 37221
615-972-8402
e-mail: tfields@fieldspublishing.com

Contents

INTRODUCTION

A Christmas Star– 1996 Albuquerque

I was so excited that I could hardly sit still long enough for my sister to comb my hair and help me with my halo; I kept turning to admire myself in our large bedroom mirror. Finally I was ready, and we all trooped down the street to Sandia Baptist Church. Soon the program began, and when the time came, I carefully wheeled myself forward and sang the first verse of *O Little Town of Bethlehem* all by myself.

It sounds ordinary enough. But it wasn't. For me to be able to participate in that Christmas program, the men of the church had to build a ramp up to the worship platform sturdy enough to support my electric wheelchair. One of the mothers figured out a way

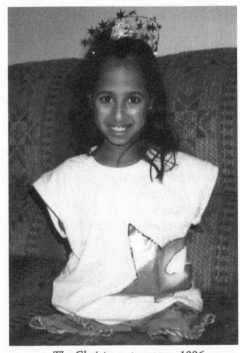

The Christmas program, 1996

to make a pair of jeans fit me, even though I had no legs. Someone else hemmed the shirt sleeves to accommodate my two inch arms and sewed a large silver star onto the front. Add to that the fact that we weren't even members of Sandia, and you begin to see how special this was.

My mom is kind of an unusual parent. She's a single woman who adopted five girls, three of them disabled, from Haiti, India and Brazil. She is a Christian who believes that children ought to know Jesus, and also to experience how believers within different denominations worship Him. She insists that there is really only one Lord, one faith, one body of Christ. So although every Sunday we went to St. Michael and All Angels Episcopal Church, when summer came we also attended VBS programs in many different churches. Since Sandia Baptist was close enough that I could "walk," I also got to participate in AWANA during the school year. When I heard plans for the Christmas musical program, I simply announced that I wanted to be in it. And so I was.

All I really remember of that night is that I was a heavenly star, one of a whole bunch of "stars" bearing the good news of Jesus' birth to the audience. My friend, Cory, stood next to me, her black curls bouncing. But when I drove myself forward to the microphone alone for my solo, I suddenly felt as if I were the only person on the platform. I don't think I was scared, but I do remember feeling awe. I grinned at the pianist, and started to sing. Every time anyone asks me to give my testimony, I think of that night, the first time I proclaimed the gospel with my voice.

This book is my story, and God's, but it is also yours. My disability, which is my particular weakness, has become the place where God's strength is victorious, just as Scripture promises. But all of our lives are like that, whoever we are.

It is good sometimes, to just stop and notice how God has shaped our lives for a particular purpose, and given us Himself by grace. That's how I hope you will read this – as an invitation to look back and see your own life as God's unique gift to the world.

CHAPTER ONE

There Was a Little Girl...

To understand why my story is both as ordinary and as unique as your own, it may help to know a little about the family into which I was adopted at 22 months of age. Maybe you remember this little rhyme:

> There was a little girl, who had a little curl,
> right in the middle of her forehead.
> And when she was good, she was very, very good,
> but when she was bad she was horrid.

My grandpa loved to tease my mother about this verse. Many years ago, when my almost two-year-old mom repeated that rhyme, she said, "but when she was bad she was horridge." She had confused the word with porridge from her favorite story of Goldilocks! Grandpa was still amused sixty three years later when he told me about it.

When my mom playfully recited it to me a few months after I arrived home in 1990 (and I did have a little curl, right in the middle of my forehead), I used to grin at her and finish it with, "but when she was bad she was bore-id." It was just funny to me, since I barely understood English, and I also thought I was saying it right. But mom figured out pretty quickly that my version was probably true. It was always a good idea to keep me busy, since I definitely did not enjoy being bore-id! Although I was nearly two, I couldn't walk, or even sit up without support, so I wasn't yet able to really entertain myself very well.

And besides, I was used to a whole bunch of other children in the same room, and caregivers playing with me all the time. My transition from pampered baby in a busy, and quite wonderful children's home in India to toddler in an ordinary American family took some adjustment! Fortunately, God provided a whole house full of sisters ready to welcome me into their family.

Becca

My oldest sister, Becca, was fifteen when I came to the States. It wasn't long before she made herself my entertainment manager. Since I didn't switch my sleeping pattern for weeks after we got home, I stayed awake when everyone else went to bed. Often, I called for somebody to play with me in the middle of the night. Pretty quickly Becky decided I was bright enough to use the VCR, so she took it upon herself to teach me to push the buttons with my little arm so I could play, rewind and replay The Little Mermaid, my favorite movie. After that, I was content to watch the adventures of Ariel and let my sisters sleep. Becca tells me that every one of the girls memorized the whole movie because I played it so often!

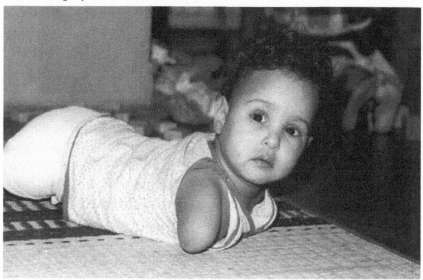

Ashraya Children's Home, 1989

Becca served as a sort of second mother to me. She likes to tell how I once flipped myself up out of my booster seat where I was supposed to be looking at a picture book and belly-flopped right onto the dining room table where she was doing her high school homework. I demanded attention by rolling right over whatever papers and books she had spread out in front of her, insisting that it was time to play, "Now, please!" It cracked her up, and soon she abandoned her study to amuse me for a while. That seems to have become a pattern. Becca loved little kids, plain and simple and always. There's never yet been a baby who didn't feel safe with her.

Becca was dying when my mom first saw her on a sunny afternoon in 1975, after having translated all day for a group of American Mennonite doctors. She had gone to Haiti a year earlier to help out in a Church of God in Christ orphanage, but rapidly got involved with all kinds of people. The Mennonites had organized a free, day-long medical clinic near the old city of St. Marc, and needed mom to help them interview patients. The lines were still long, late on that November day, and everyone was getting tired. Because she could speak the best Creole, my mom, who was also a nurse, had gone outside to try to triage the remaining patients to identify the sickest ones who would need to be seen before the doctors returned to Port-au-Prince. When she saw Becca, she hesitated. The child that the sad-eyed young woman held out to her was so thin mom could see its heart beating. It wasn't medicine that infant needed, it was food. Haiti had suffered a long drought, and many malnourished, orange-haired children had passed through the clinic that day already. The doctors and nurses had given them vitamins, worm medicine and whatever food was available. Still, my mom hadn't seen any babies as close to death as this one. She reached out to gather the little one in her arms.

A Haitian pastor stepped up beside her and warned, "If you take her and she dies, people will blame the Christians." So, reluctantly, my mother turned away and the tiny girl's eight-year-old cousin carried her back home to die. Darkness had fallen when mom and the others finally boarded the truck for the long ride back toward town. But as they traveled in the moonlight, mom and her best Haitian

8

friend began to realize that they had listened to the voice of caution, and not the voice of God. So early the next morning, the two women retraced their steps having enlisted the help of an American missionary who owned a small truck. After they finally located the baby in a tiny thatch-roofed house, my mom wrapped Becca up in a blanket and carried her back to her own house to try to keep her alive. At first mom had to use an eye dropper to give Becca small amounts of weak formula. Mom kept her warm in a narrow cardboard box that had once been used to display packets of vegetable seeds. Hardly anyone expected her new baby to live. But miraculously, Becca gained weight, thrived and delighted everyone around her with her energy and enthusiasm.

My mom is independent. Cathy Cox, RN, had a whole bunch of things she wanted to do in her life. She never planned to marry and she didn't plan to adopt children. But once her eyes met Becca's, she wasn't about to abandon "her" baby. She soon discovered that Becca's mother had died a month earlier, and that there was no one left to nurse her. The villagers had nicknamed her ti fil fer ("thin little piece of wire") which, when I look at the photos is about what she was. Mom gave her the name Rebecca, for the gutsy and courageous woman of Genesis, and Grace, because it seemed she was God's gift to my mom. And so she is, but not just to her. Becca herself has adopted six children, and is a fantastic mother to them. She's courageous, too, loving them day by day despite the fact that Becca has struggled with pain and multiple surgeries related to the Crohn's disease she's had since she was a teenager. Becca is still the big sister I look up to, a great friend, and my most enthusiastic cheerleader.

Shanti

I hadn't been home long before mom discovered how much I wanted to draw. She let me scribble all over the plastic table on my baby walker with Crayola markers gripped between my teeth. The colors made me laugh aloud, and I loved making wiggly lines with them. But I wanted to sing while I scribbled, or to chat, and it frustrated me not to be able to do both at once. My sister, Shanti, also from India, was nearby. She was eight at the time. Shanti is legally blind and mentally handicapped, but she squatted on the floor beside me all afternoon, taking each marker when I was finished with it and patiently handing me another. She watched what I was doing. She knew I was annoyed with having to be quiet when I tried to draw. And she figured out a solution. She dragged out some sponges my mom had under the kitchen sink, cut them in half, poked a hole in each one and then shoved a marker in each piece of sponge. She taught me to hold the sponge between my shoulder and chin, and soon I could sing and make a mess on the plastic table at the same time! My mom was astonished. So were my other sisters. Shanti kept working on her project, nagging my mom for better and softer sponges which she cut up until they fit me perfectly. I used those sponges for months until I could hold the markers, crayons and pencils securely without them.

My mom adopted Shanti from "my" orphanage. Born in 1982, she'd arrived as a noisy, distracted four-year-old who couldn't see well or hear clearly. Shanti had only a little vision in her "good" eye and for a long time she was also almost totally deaf, due to long-standing and stubborn infections. Her eardrums had to be surgically re-created after she had been in the States for a year or so. She is also intellectually disabled, with an IQ of about 70, but Shanti is creative, kind and thoughtful – fully alive.

She had originally wanted a "pink" eye, Shanti told me, when mom arranged for her prosthetic one. Failing to get that, she sometimes picked real flowers to shove into her empty eye socket in order to be beautiful. But the brown eye she eventually wore turned out to be just as good for her purposes. Shanti is a tease, and if the mood struck her, she'd just take out her eye and chase other kids with it! Once she dropped it under the swings, and since she couldn't see well enough to locate it by herself, the whole school spent an hour searching before somebody finally found it. Shanti rinsed off her sand-covered eye and cheerfully popped it back in. Sweet and sensitive, she was always happy to cuddle me, play with me, sneak Girl Scout cookies out of the freezer for me, and watch any movie I wanted, no matter how many times she'd seen it before.

As an adult she has struggled. Not many people find it easy to befriend someone who can't keep up with them intellectually. She has been manipulated and taken advantage of because she trusts easily. And there are very few jobs left in our technological culture for the many mildly retarded people who can manage pretty well on their own, but whose disability means that opportunities for real employment are limited. Her name means "peace" and it seems to me that she has given more of it than she has received. I love her.

Jaya

Because I was the youngest, I inherited everybody else's baby dolls as the girls outgrew them. I dragged those dolls around like any other little girl, but I couldn't dress or undress my many babies. Although I liked to sing to them, read to a troop of dolls lined up by my bed, or pretend to feed them with a little spoon, I didn't actually enjoy playing with dolls very much.

But being the "doll" was a whole other thing. My big sister Jaya, seven and in first grade when I arrived, treated me like a favorite toy. She liked to dress me up in ridiculous clothes, feed me, and get Shanti to put me in the doll carriage and parade me around. Jaya couldn't lift me herself, even though I hardly weighed anything, but she loved to comb my hair, adding barrettes and whatever ribbons she could find. She was beautiful and bossy, and when she wanted to be, she was also a whole lot of fun.

Our Jayanthi ("the victorious one") had come home from Calcutta at age four, unable to walk because of a spinal cord birth defect, spina bifida. She had been described as a "chirpy kid," which my mom took to mean that she had a bubbly personality. Indeed she did! Jaya was talkative, full of laughter and giggles. She was slowed down only by contractures of both hips, paralysis of her legs, and club feet. But according to the stories I've heard, Jaya was able to get anywhere she wanted to go. After she had a couple of surgeries at the Shriner's hospital in Los Angeles, she wore long leg braces and could walk with crutches. Until she learned to catheterize herself she wore diapers, which she hated, but woe to any kid who teased her about it. Her kindergarten teacher found Jaya once standing face to face with a little boy she'd backed up against the playground fence, threatening him with a crutch, which she wielded like a night stick.

Jaya's early life was painful. When she was little, she had been abandoned outside a hospital where many families milled about, even overnight. It was a day or two before the police finally realized she was alone. No one knows why her family felt they had to leave her there. But by the time she was rescued, she had stopped talking. For the next year she languished in an orphanage for mentally retarded children, until a social worker realized she understood everything that was said to her. Transferred to a different home for normal children, she began to speak and to make progress again. But that early loss and sense of rejection hurt her deeply, and she continued to struggle all through her childhood and adolescence, often angry and desperate for the acceptance she could never believe was real, even when it was freely and consistently given by so many. Life has not been easy for her, despite her beauty and her brains. Eventually she moved to California with her little girl, Jasmine, a beauty who looks just like Jaya. Today I am remembering her laughter, and hoping that she'll come through the door one of these days, eager to tell us everything she's achieved.

Debbie

During that first year, I didn't see much of my fourteen-year-old sister, Debbie. Mom had adopted her from Brazil when she was eight, just a year younger than Becca. In fact, Becca traveled with my mom to Brazil to bring Debbie to the States. By then, Debbie had suffered a lot, maybe more than any of my sisters. She had lived in several different orphanages, which meant she never was able to attach to any permanent caregiver. Stubborn and fiercely independent, she thought she didn't need any parenting at all, and when anybody crossed her, she could become violent. It was after she had grabbed Jaya by the hair and thrown her against a wall that mom finally took her to the children's psychiatric hospital, where she was still living when I arrived.

Debbie had plenty of reasons to be angry. Besides being abandoned, she'd been repeatedly sexually abused in a home where she had been sent as a maid, sometime during the year before my mom adopted her. She had finally demanded to be returned to the orphanage, where she waited to see if anyone would want her. Mom did. After that betrayal, Debbie was suspicious of all adults, and didn't trust anybody at all. Her tantrums were legendary. Everyone was afraid of how she'd react to me. In fact, she had threatened to throw me down the stairs.

However, Debbie turned out to be a special friend to me. Maybe because she'd been hurt so badly herself, she felt I might be rejected, too, and she always watched out for me. She was able to love me freely and easily, perhaps because there was no way I could ever hurt her. And she was smart. There wasn't a game Debbie didn't know, or a project she wasn't ready to undertake. She had learned English rapidly, and used her considerable imagination to make up exciting stories and games. Debbie could be really funny, and has grown up to be a good mom to her own girls.

When she was good, she was very, very good! When she was bad she was dangerous. That's true of all human beings, I think. We are all individuals, but we are all so much the same. Sin and grace are both ordinary. Everybody struggles, and everybody is sometimes very, very good and, sometimes, horrid. That's why the verse is funny. It fits us all.

Each one of us brought our own histories into this new family. My mom struggled and failed and sometimes succeeded, right along with the rest of us. Sometimes she was even "horridge!" None of us was exactly perfect. Love isn't easy. Forgiveness is hard. What each child had experienced before being adopted impacted everyone else. Some emotional hurts aren't ever healed in this life. We didn't always know what to do to help each other, but mom never gave up on us, or on herself, and she never let us give up either. She used to say, "This is the only family we've got. Nobody gets to choose a different one," which is another way of telling the truth. Life isn't fair, nobody's perfect, and we're all happier once we accept that reality.

CHAPTER TWO

The Blue Blanket

My mom spent several days at the children's home in India before flying back to Albuquerque with me in February, 1990. I don't remember that trip, of course, although she recalls it vividly. It stretched out to many hours, and the temperature inside the aircraft was freezing cold. Early during the flight, mom had covered me up with a passenger blanket. I snuggled down into it and fell asleep in her arms for most of the journey across the ocean.

New York was even colder than the plane had been, and we didn't have any winter clothes. Everything she'd brought for me had been checked through to New Mexico. So when mom carried me off the plane in early February, anticipating a very long layover, one of the stewardesses told her to keep the blanket. The gift of the blue blanket was intended to be purely practical, but Mom soon discovered that I had already become attached to that soft American Airlines blanket. It was small, for one thing, just my size. I clung to it summer and winter, even when the temperature didn't require its warmth. For years, it was my favorite "blankie," and I always kept it on my bed. During those many hours crossing from one side of the world to the other, it had taken on new meaning. It wasn't just a means of keeping me warm. That blue blanket meant love and security. It meant everything was going to be all right. It meant my mother's arms. Wisely, my mom let me hang on to it through every move. I still have that threadbare little blanket!

Ordinary objects can become powerful symbols when they are attached to something or someone that really matters to us. I know how much it helped me to grow up in a family where symbols, even simple ones like my blue blanket, were acknowledged to be powerful, and where their significance was at the same time both mysterious and explicit. We experienced the power of symbol most visibly during holiday seasons.

When Advent came to New Mexico, one of my sisters dragged a large, bare tree branch into the house, where we planted it firmly in a big pot of dirt. Then, night after night we took turns reading a Bible story, beginning with God's creation of the world all the way up to Jesus' birth in Bethlehem. Finally, one of us hung a special ornament on the dead branch.

The Jesse Tree takes its name from Isaiah 11:1: "A shoot shall come out of from the stump of Jesse, and a branch shall grow out of his roots." In this chapter, Isaiah begins a wonderful, long section about God's intention to finally and fully redeem His people. Jesse, of course, was the father of King David. Although that line of Davidic kings had been destroyed by Isaiah's time, he announced that the "root" of Jesse was still alive, and that the long dead stump would one day bring forth a shoot that would live forever. The New Testament interprets this "root" as Jesus, son of David and son of God, the eternal king above all kings.

From the time Becca was little, she (and then all my older sisters) made a few new ornaments each year, slowly replacing the commercially prepared set mom had originally bought. She laminated each carefully crayoned, pasted or painted symbol, so that they would last. Completely original, our biblical story-pictures also included more women than the old set had provided, people like Rahab and Deborah. That mattered because we were a house full of girls, and Mom wanted us to see ourselves in the Bible's story. On the back of each ornament I can still read who made it and when, plus the Bible reference to the story it represents. Every Advent night for all my life we have read the stories aloud and hung the ornaments.

To the bewilderment of our neighbors, we didn't put up our Christmas tree until the afternoon of Christmas Eve. It was always a fresh evergreen, sweet smelling, forever-alive, and soon it became even more gorgeous as my mom slowly added string after string of lights. Those two symbols, juxtaposed right against each other, showed me that no matter what, eventually God keeps His promises. Those symbols also pointed me to the everlasting beauty of the Word, the true Light, the shoot of Jesse – Jesus, the Lord.

To unbelievers who have never seen one or heard the Christmas story, the traditional manger scene doesn't mean anything at all. It has significance only for those who fill it with glad story-meaning like we did. Because ours took so long to create, and because each year it was different, the busy village, the tired woman traveling to Bethlehem with her husband, and our unrecognized Savior born in a stable became deeply personal to us.

When Becca was a baby and my mom still lived in Haiti, she bought a whole lot of little Haitian figurines made of wood, cloth and wire. They show Haitian men and women carrying fruit on their heads, riding donkeys, sweeping, buying vegetables, playing drums and just standing around. Instead of the traditional manger scene she didn't have, she turned those figures into Mary, Joseph, shepherds, wise men, and a whole village full of people going about their ordinary lives. After she brought Becca home, she kept all those figures. Over the years she added other small dolls representing many cultures and countries, tiny sheep, small baskets and little pieces of pottery. She wanted to us to see that the whole world belonged there in Bethlehem, and that Jesus had been born for everybody, everywhere.

Every year we were allowed to use those little figures to construct a whole new scene. It could take us days, as we arranged and rearranged our handiwork. Sometimes we made a barn of rough wood, or a cave of rocks behind Bethlehem, where Mary and Joseph would finally rest on Christmas Eve. We had time to work on it, and we took time. The fact that Bethlehem was a bustling village said a lot to me, even then. In historical reality, hardly anyone noticed when Jesus was born in Bethlehem of Judea. The coming of Christ as a human baby wasn't recognized, let alone celebrated, except by foreign star-gazers and dirty shepherds. Hardly anyone knew to watch for Him, and all the inns were full. When we sang, "O come, to my heart, Lord Jesus, there is room in my heart for thee," I thought of that.

One year I had read a short children's book, The Glass Mermaid by Susan Clymer, about a little girl, a special ornament and the grandfather who had given it to her. I loved that story, and the idea of a glass mermaid coming to life enchanted me. So I begged my mom for one. These days she could probably go online and find such a thing in half an hour, but before the internet she had to scour store after store. When she couldn't find a glass mermaid, she settled on a brightly painted metal one that is still precious to me. It reminds me of the story, it reminds me of my mother's persistent love, and it reminds me of my early desire to be as free to move through my world as a mermaid does in hers. It's a real symbol now, not just a piece of colored tin.

She also bought a new Christmas story book every year. Many of those have become family favorites, and every winter mom still reads them all aloud, now to Becca's children, and even to me. We never tire of them. Stories like Apple Tree Christmas by Trinka Hakes Noble, The Trees of the Dancing Goats by Patricia Polacco, and Jenny and the Black Stocking by Jane Belk Moncure, spell out the heart of Christmas in wonderful ways. The Miracle of St. Nicholas by Gloria Whelan, Farolitos for Christmas by Rudolfo Anaya, Probity Jones and the Fear Not Angel by Walter Wangerin, and my personal favorite, a story of World War 1 Poland, The Bell-Ringer of Pinsk by Eric P. Kelly, make themselves wholly at home in a child's heart, especially if that child hears them repeatedly.

Without preaching, such rich tales became part of what Christmas means. They, too, are fuller than they seem at first reading. Our books come by way of many different cultures, nations and traditions. Jesus belongs to the whole world, and everywhere Christians celebrate the same event differently, yet all of them rightly. Each new story contributed to our embrace of the glory of "God in flesh appearing," a mystery that is knowable, but always beyond our understanding, let alone our cultural possession!

Another symbol-rich time for us occurred during Holy Week, the week before Easter. Each day included its own important commemoration, beginning with joy as we waved real palms and sang the "loud

Hosannas!" during the Palm Sunday procession. As the week progressed, our beautiful church darkened. The flowers disappeared from the sanctuary, and everything became more solemn. We moved through the celebration of the Last Supper on Thursday and the story of Jesus' betrayal by Judas, and finally on Friday, we heard the terrible long story of Jesus' trial. We sat still as He carried His own cross, and stood silent as the deacon read of His death on the cross. Good Friday is the darkest day and the longest service. For a child, it can seem as if the whole world might really die right then with Jesus. It moved me deeply, even as a little girl. There were no happy songs that day.

I knew that Jesus is forever alive. I hadn't learned to sing "Jesus loves the little children" for nothing. But still, I was in the pew beside my mom crying when Brian Taylor, our priest, left the church after the service. He stopped to reassure me, "Jesus isn't really dead now, Minda," he said. I was barely five that spring, but quite indignant, and when I looked up at him I retorted loudly enough for others to hear, "I know that, but right now He is."

It is natural for a child to understand that we live in a universe where the past is also present, and the future is already near. Jesus was alive, is alive, of course. But right then, I was "seeing" his death. And both were true. I am glad we didn't just skip over that, or hide it under too-early Easter festivities.

Of course, Easter is the absolute center of Christian celebration, and for us, it continues a long time long beyond Sunday itself, glorious as that is. The Easter season lasts all the way until Pentecost. This meant we had a whole six weeks of Easter, so we kept right on singing resurrection hymns, repeating all the alleluias and even dyeing Easter eggs and finding treats, week after week. Those, too, were living symbols, rich with meaning. The story of Jesus' victory over death was kept fresh in our hearts and ears and eyes, day after day.

That same spring, my favorite pre-school classmate called me excitedly a week before Easter to tell me that his cat had produced a litter of kittens. Mom agreed that I could have one. Carefully I chose a soft grey and white female and named her Emily. The kittens were small enough and light enough that I could actually hold them. Emily seemed to know she was mine and never struggled to get away, but curled up against my shoulder and purred a contented kitten purr.

I was supposed to bring Emily home a few days before Pentecost, but one morning Bela's mom called mine to say that Bela had tripped and fallen on top of Emily. My kitten was barely breathing, and her back legs didn't work. Bela felt awful, and when we got to his house, he was crying. Convinced that Emily was going to be just fine, I didn't shed a tear. I understood what everyone told me, I just didn't believe them. I just rocked my limp little Emily against my neck, crooning softly to her. Our parents were worried. When mom finally grew exasperated and told me directly that my kitten was dying, I looked up at her in bewildered astonishment and said, "But Mom, nothing dies at Easter!"

In fact, Emily grew fat and sassy and came home to me perfectly-healthy several weeks later. I had heard the Easter story, and seen it acted out in the liturgy that took us from darkness to light, from sorrow to joy, from death to life. When it mattered, I made my own application about the power of the resurrection. It was all very real to me.

In those days our mother tried to help us understand the deep meanings hidden in the visible symbols of faith. We missed a lot of it then, but I don't think she cared. There was always next year. She figured that if we celebrated these holy mysteries over and over we would eventually embrace their power. She was right.

Symbols, no matter whether they are as small and personal as a baby blanket or as globally significant as the cross, are shorthand for our best God-stories. They help us to remember what matters most to us. When we do, "We bring the original power of a past event into the present," as my mom would say. We decide what matters most to us, what events we want to remember forever, and what is important enough to celebrate.

But here is another truth for ordinary people like us—if we cling to symbols of our disappointments and doubts, holding tightly to what we recall of pain, loss or bitterness, then the dark power of those past events will also enter in to affect our present. Choose carefully.

CHAPTER THREE

Wheels, Arms and Legs

Because I had no legs, I especially loved the sea creatures that moved without them – fish, sharks, dolphins and mermaids. The Little Mermaid came out when I was little and it quickly became my favorite movie. The first time I saw seals at the zoo I demanded to stay still and watch them swim, staring at them playing and rolling in the water, unwilling to pull myself away. I had never seen anything so beautiful. If there hadn't been a glass wall between us, I'd have tried to get into the water with them. Those creatures had freedom to move anywhere, and I did not. I don't remember this part, but my mom said that after a while I looked at her and softly breathed, "Mommy, look. They're just like me."

But soon a sort of freedom came to me, too. It was bright, and it was hot pink, my favorite color. Most importantly, it was mine. I was only three, and not everyone was sure I could manage it, but I giggled with delight when my mom lifted me into my new Barbie wheelchair. I pushed the black joystick with my little arm, tentatively at first, and then with more confidence as I sat high above the ground and moved myself across the room for the first time.

Now I could see what other kids my age saw when they climbed on chairs. The change in perspective was thrilling. I could drive my chair up to any window and look outside whenever I wanted to. I could even get myself up close to the stove and see the knobs and the burners and the hamburgers frying in the pan. My mom showed me how to crack eggs, and then let me help scramble them. It was wonderful.

My chair could also go fast, a sensation that was both new and exciting. The fact that for a long time I didn't bother to watch where I was going made my early excursions outdoors harrowing for others to watch, but I was having the time of my life. Despite my mom's fears, I never did tip off the sidewalk or get hit by a car. I discovered something else, too. My wheelchair was the envy of the neighborhood preschoolers. No one else had anything like it. "Barbie" made me something of a celebrity, definitely not a child needing to be pitied or avoided. When I blazed out in that pink chair, other kids begged for rides!

But I still needed to be "fixed." Everyone agreed with that. The fact that I didn't have limbs seemed to be a serious issue to professionals. Even the children's home in India wanted to know when I was going to get arms and legs. Since I longed, no, begged for shoes, my mom had a prosthetist make me simple legs just after my fourth birthday. They turned out to be useful for nothing at all. Yes, I could stand, which gave me a sense of being a "big girl." When I stood up I was suddenly tall. But I still couldn't walk, because I had no way to balance myself or to use crutches. The legs were uncomfortable because my partially formed feet had to be squished into them at a weird angle. But yes, I could wear overalls, tights with dresses, and especially, I could wear cool shoes. I remember them now with perfect joy – pink tennis shoes and white leather sandals! I really, really loved them. Driving my wheelchair around with legs made an unbelievable difference in the way other people saw me. Even without arms, I seemed somehow more like a whole person to them.

A year or so later, the prosthetist tried several different systems to hold my new, hard plastic arms in place over my little stumps so that I could use my back muscles to open and close the hooks that served for hands. Although I rather liked the idea of having arms, and definitely enjoyed the attention I got when I wore them, my carefully constructed arms never did work very well. They got in my way and slowed me down. I couldn't dress myself or get in or out of my wheelchair by myself when I had them on. Even driving "Barbie" was harder. I couldn't lift anything as easily as I could when I just balanced the weight between my shoulder and neck. The wires on the elbows got caught in my dresses, and the weight of my new arms pulled me forward and made it harder to sit upright. Worst of all, I still didn't have any fingernails to polish. If I had, that might have given me some incentive to work more happily at making those arms useful!

It is true that I could manage some things pretty easily with my hooks. As long as I treated them like toys that I could play with or not, whenever I chose, they were fine. I could certainly wear all kinds of pretty dresses more easily, without having to cut off the sleeves. I could hang on to a Popsicle stick all by myself instead of eating my treat from a saucer. And I was actually able to hold a lighted candle at the Christmas Eve service, which made me very proud. There were a few definite advantages to wearing my arms.

But it drove me crazy not to feel anything. The sense of touch was very important to me, and I missed it. I liked to feel the softness of a towel fresh out of the dryer, the cold wetness of melting snow, and the grit of sand in my sandbox. When I hugged my mom, I wanted to feel my arms against her skin. I was separated from everything when I wore prosthetics. When my arms were strapped on, I couldn't tell whether my chocolate was still too hot to drink, or whether it had cooled enough to sip it through a straw. I had no idea whether I had a good grip on a round plastic marker, and sometimes it slipped and slid all over the place before it just fell out of my grasp. And those plastic arms were hot.

Other people did treat me differently when they saw me "whole" with legs and arms. I did look more normal, and I got a lot fewer stares and rude comments. Wearing them seemed to make it easier for people to approach me, especially in stores or on the street. And I did like that. Even a little kid knows when adults are staring, and trying to pretend they aren't.

But my mom saw that when I was completely encased in all that plastic, I was miserable. Before I put the prostheses on, I could get in and out of my bed by myself, roll across the room fast, turn pages in a book, grab crayons or paint brushes, and build a tower of blocks. I could reach out and hug somebody, pick flowers, hold the phone and even play Nintendo. I could draw, use scissors and play my xylophone. I could shove things out of my way, and eat nearly anything, even soup, without spilling. I could pick up a glass of milk and put a straw in a coke. I could print legibly. I could pull myself to a sitting position from the floor without support, and even "walk," using my partial feet and hips to propel me. I could climb stairs. I felt free to do anything I wanted to do.

With my prostheses, I struggled to accomplish any of those things, even with lots of practice. Everybody had used their skills to make me less disabled. Everyone wanted to make life easier for me, but these efforts to make me "normal" made me more handicapped. How I looked mattered to me. Apparently it mattered to a lot of people who looked at me, too. But being myself was also important, and I felt like I was lost inside all that plastic. Eventually we simply threw all those arms and legs in the back of my closet. And no one ever mentioned them again. How I looked lost out to who I am. And that is a choice I have never regretted.

CHAPTER FOUR

Healing the Children

Rezarta arrived at our house when she was barely seven, just exactly my age, as blond as I was dark, as frail as I was sturdy. My new best friend had traveled from Albania to the U.S. for life-saving heart surgery unavailable in her country. We were instant friends. I loved riding her around on the back of my wheelchair so that she could "walk" outdoors, even when she was too tired to manage the distance on her own. Rezarta was polite, careful and a little shy. I was none of those things, and happily led her astray, often forgetting to tell anyone where we were going. Together we managed to find plenty of things to do, and sometimes the opportunity to get into trouble! Mostly we laughed.

Once she had recovered from surgery, Rezarta felt well for the first time in her life, and before she returned home to Tirana, Rezi was able to play hard. She would run across the park beside my chair, or jump on the bed, or climb to the top of the monkey bars. Together we splashed in the swimming pool and cuddled up to listen to my mom read a bedtime story. Somehow I thought we would be together forever. When she boarded the plane that took her far away, it was terrible for me. I had no idea of geography, how impossibly far Albania was from Albuquerque. But I knew she was gone forever. Rezarta's spirit, sparkling and courageous, had made her a terrific addition to our family. Losing her was my first conscious experience of loss and I felt it acutely. Having her with us was all gift, all joy, and I miss her still.

Rezarta wasn't our first foster child. We never had a brother, so when Roberto arrived from Guatemala for facial surgery, my sisters and I were in for a treat! Roberto was close to my age, had a wicked grin and a hilarious sense of humor. He wasn't embarrassed to play house, or to dress himself up as a witch, complete with huge pointy black hat drooping down over his ears. Mostly deaf, he didn't care what language we used, but he loved Nintendo as much as I did, a game I could actually play pretty well. We were crazy competitors, and he kept us laughing.

There were many others, but one little boy especially won our hearts. My mom carried Hugo into the house in the middle of the night. Exhausted, he didn't wake up until late the next morning, and then it was to see several of us peering into his crib. He should have been terrified, but he wasn't. Barely two, with a mop of curly blond hair and sparkling brown eyes, Hugo was adorable, plain and simple. He required several complex surgeries, and remained with us for many months. Hugo definitely became our "baby," glorying in the practically constant attention of five older sisters. Becca still keeps a photo of Hugo on the wall of her home, along with pictures of her own six adopted children.

My sisters and I had come to the States from Brazil, Haiti and India. Mom thought we ought to know that there were plenty of other children in need all over the world, and that together we had the privilege of making life better for some of them. She was determined not to let us think that we were somehow the center of the universe because we had been adopted, or because we had suffered, or because we had disabilities. So our family fostered children for the organization Healing the Children. We cared for the little ones who lived with us for several months at a time, but having them also helped to heal us of self-absorption. We all had to deal with children moving in and out of our house, sharing our rooms and our stuff, speaking other languages, bringing new challenges and new joys. Our world kept expanding, and that helped to widen our hearts, too.

We learned quite a lot about sick children who needed help that wasn't easily available where they lived. We also discovered that sometimes their problems were so serious that even our best doctors couldn't heal them, like the beautiful baby girl who flew to us from

Haiti for a medical evaluation. Sadly, she returned home to her village without surgery, because no medical intervention could cure her. I thought about that for a long time.

My mom inspired me to reach out to other people, just as she did. But it was all just so ordinary. She didn't make any big production of it. I'm sure these experiences played a significant role in preparing me to hear my cross-cultural calling many years later. I know for sure that they made me understand that my own disability, although it sometimes made my life difficult, was really No Big Deal.

It's not that my mom wasn't busy enough with her nursing job, home schooling me, and raising all five of us girls. She was; but she was also looking far down the road at our future, at the kind of people she hoped we would become. Besides, she didn't even try to do it all alone. Mom was forever bringing interesting people into our lives. She specifically urged us to collect as many other "mothers" as we could find. Those caring adults taught us all sorts of things and gave us loads of attention.

Each of us had our particular favorites, of course. One of mine was a nurse at the homecare agency where mom worked. She was Jewish, born in Argentina. Graciela won my heart immediately because she was so much fun. I was especially enchanted by her accent, which I tried to mimic. To her everlasting credit Graciela thought I was perfect, even when I most emphatically was not!

Of course, we invited Graciela to celebrate Hanukkah with us. She got right down on the floor to play games, while my mom made latkes in the kitchen. I was only two when she first came, and couldn't exactly spin the dreidel on the floor like my sisters, but I still wanted my chance to win some chocolate gelt. After watching for a while, I figured out how to throw the little wooden top off my shoulder so that it fell to the floor spinning. Graciela was delighted. She was proud when I stubbornly insisted on taking my turn lighting the candles on our menorah, using a long fireplace match to do it.

But why were we Christians celebrating Hanukkah in the first place? Mom had traveled to Amsterdam many years before, and while she was there, she found a heavy, old brass menorah in the back of a dusty second-hand store, bought it and brought it home. Every year we lit the candles one by one, and the tiny flames shone through the living room window where it stood. When I was a few years older, mom told me that the menorah we carefully polished each winter had once been the precious possession of a family whose belongings, and maybe even whose lives, had been lost during the Holocaust. Every year we remembered them without knowing their names, and we kindled the Hanukkah lights in their place so that the flame of their faith would not die. It was solemn. And it was beautiful.

I realized then that terrible things can happen to God's people. I saw that God hadn't "fixed" anything for the Jews when Nazis raided their homes and herded whole families off to the gas chambers. But I knew, too, that God had been with each of them even then, because God cannot be kept out of any place, no matter how evil it is. The part of God's story that the Jews found themselves living through during those terrible years seemed to be the end of their story. But in the end, an end that so many millions of Jews never saw with their own eyes, it was the Nazis whose kingdom was destroyed, not God's.

Slowly I came to realize why my mom chose to honor the faith of an ordinary family who trusted in God, even when God didn't rescue them from suffering and death. Our menorah symbolized God's faithfulness even when His silence must have looked like abandonment. It strengthened me to understand that no matter what, I didn't need to be afraid to trust God either. We don't see everything. Sometimes we don't see anything. God is just who God is. And that is enough.

I'm glad my mom let us help with Healing the Children. We needed to see our own capacity for relieving the loneliness and homesickness of those children, even though we ourselves were struggling to find our place. Allowing us to see pain and to ease it, gave us a sense of our own power to make a difference. It taught us, little by little, to look beyond our circumstances to God's future, where every tear will be wiped away.

A quote from one of my favorite contemporary movies makes the same point. A Hindu young man, the hero of the movie, says, "Everything will be all right in the end. If it's not all right, then it's not yet the end" (The Best Exotic Marigold Hotel).

27

CHAPTER FIVE

Traveling Companions

I had only been in New Mexico for a little while when we took a family vacation to visit one of my mom's Nazarene Seminary professors in Missouri. It was a miserable winter, even though it was officially spring break. On a cold afternoon, our van hit a patch of ice and slid off the road into a snow-filled ditch. Becca remembers it better than anyone. I was in the back of the van with her and temporarily out of my car seat since she had been changing my diaper. She grabbed on to me and everyone else screamed as we started down the embankment. I broke the tension when I shouted quite unexpectedly, "Hang on, everybody!" Since I'd never said anything like that before, my sisters and my mom all cracked up laughing. And they hung on. Soon a tow truck appeared to pull us out, and it wasn't long before we were back on the road again. That was unusual, but road trips were always adventures. We hardly ever knew what we would do, or see, or experience along the way.

Shanti and Jaya hated those long drives and generally bickered with each other over crayons, whose turn it was to choose where we should stop for lunch or over nothing at all. I liked to go anywhere, winter or summer. I could see for a long way off while enthroned in my car seat. I distinctly remember imagining that the mountains were bowing down to us as we drove through them on the way to Colorado or Utah, and that we were welcomed and sheltered by their power. I loved that feeling. I learned a lot, too, because if Shanti and Jaya got to arguing too much, mom would just start quizzing them on math facts, state capitals, or Bible stories, which she figured was at least a productive form of competition. Becca and Debbie had blank outline maps of the U.S. and fought with each other to be the first to see an unfamiliar license plate.

Whenever we stopped for a break, Becca would pick me up and we would wander away from our sisters. More than anyone, she knew I wanted to explore. Sometimes she helped me touch an especially smooth wall or feel the roughness of a brick one. Even though I couldn't actually get anywhere by myself when I was out of my wheelchair, she helped me do it. Becca lifted me up onto high rocks when the others climbed them, held me out so I could pet friendly dogs, and even put me down into a stream of cold mountain water so I could feel what it was like. Because of her eagerness to introduce me to new things, I was able to experience the world a little bit more like other children do. She made every outing an adventure.

But even mom was not always predictable. Without warning, she might turn down some narrow dirt road for a better view of the canyon lands, or follow a sign to some unexplored monument, or notice a small town fair. She might suddenly pull off the highway at a homemade stand where an old woman was selling watermelon, peaches, or Navajo fry bread. Whenever that happened, we all trooped out and she would buy us a treat and offer us an opportunity to talk to someone new. I never wondered what those vendors thought of me because no one in our family paid much attention to anyone's skin color or disability. I don't remember that mom ever offered any explanation about us. No matter where we went, we just acted like what we were – an ordinary family.

We often traveled to see our grandparents. By the time I was adopted, Grandpa and Grandma had a large old house in Mount Pleasant, Utah, one with an interesting circular staircase and lots of rooms. In retirement, they volunteered full time at Wasatch Academy, a Presbyterian boarding school, and the oldest high school in the state. My grandpa ran the library and tutored international students in English. He was a genius and I adored him. "If you ask Clifford Cox what time it is," the students teased, "he'll tell you how to make a clock!" It was funny, but there was truth in it. Actually, if you asked him the time, he might also want to talk about what "time" is, why we might want to measure it, and how sundials and water clocks work. He seemed to know everything – history as well as physics, chemistry and accounting, musicology and gunsmithing. He even taught a few interested high school students how to make their own violas and guitars, leading them through the whole process from selecting the wood all the way to stringing the finished instrument. He explains why my mom is such an avid reader as well, why she is hopelessly curious about everything, and why she doesn't settle for easy answers to anything at all.

I adored my grandpa. He loved us. I remember hot summer evenings when we sat around and roasted marshmallows in their enormous fireplace, just because we wanted to, even though it made the house even hotter. I moved close enough to watch how he placed old newspapers between the carefully arranged logs. Best of all, I loved to see the paper catch fire and then slowly creep up to burn the small twigs, then the larger sticks and finally the logs. Sometimes he put me on his knee and held me so that I could light the fire myself. Together we stared at the flames. He never seemed to be in a hurry. He didn't say a lot, either. We just sat together. Finally, after a long time, when the logs had burned down enough for roasting marshmallows, he held my arm steady as I speared the marshmallow and balanced the heavy metal stick between my arm and chin. When I dropped one in the fire, he just smiled and got me another.

My grandpa died not long ago at age 94. He had moved next door to my mom and I in Bolivar after my grandma died, and so we got to enjoy him every day. He was frail and nearly blind, but in the last years before he died, Grandpa helped me get through both College Algebra and Meteorology, because neither was the least bit mysterious to him. He always enjoyed teaching me what he loved, and he seemed to love it all. When I was in Botswana for six months during my junior year at SBU, he waited for mom to read him every letter and tried to see every photo. Grandpa was proud of me, and I knew it. When I returned home, sad and already homesick for my new country, he was also the one who urged me to finish college happily instead of wishing

30

I were back in Botswana, and to stop pining for the country and people I had come to love. It was important to him to convey that to me, and he did gently, but seriously. That was the last lengthy and carefully prepared lecture he gave me before he became too ill to talk. He taught me so much, including how to become old and frail, and to die gracefully. My grandpa is my hero.

When I was a little girl, my grandma ran the thrift store in one of the old buildings on the Wasatch Academy campus. The store served many rural poor families in the area but it also became our favorite shopping center. Crammed with everything from Christmas tree ornaments to books, from clothing of all kinds to kitchen utensils, it was magical, always mysterious. Every year my sisters found beautiful things to add to their wardrobes as they rummaged through discarded student clothing that cost us practically nothing. I spent a lot of time on the floor checking out whatever I could find in the children's area. Sometimes my grandma would put a dress, or a toy she thought I'd like down on the very bottom shelf, hidden behind long sleeve shirts or pajamas that she knew I'd immediately push away. It was a kind of game and I loved it. I discovered pretty early that what was visible to my eye was not always all there was, or the best there was, so I learned to look harder and to dig deeper.

Of course she understood how hard it was to find clothing that really fit me, especially as I got older. One summer I was in the store after I'd learned to sit up and "walk" around, when something hanging on the rack directly above me caught my eye. I remember so well how I longed for that sky-blue dress with tiny pink flowers and a wide lace collar, but it had long sleeves. Grandma saw me gazing at it but didn't say a word. The next day she surprised me with that very dress, already altered to fit me. She had stayed up late to do it. I was so surprised and happy! After my mom helped me put it on, I twirled around and around in my now sleeveless, shortened dress, dancing with sheer joy.

On another occasion, during Thanksgiving when I was seven or eight, I wanted to drink my sparkling cider out of a wine glass like everyone else did. Mom was uneasy because she thought I might drop the expensive crystal or spill the juice all over the beautifully set table.

31

Grandma pulled down one of the shorter stemmed glasses, just as elegant but smaller, and let me try. I reached for it with great care and managed to drink without spilling anything. Grandma was proud. She had given me a chance to prove myself, and I had done it!

We always stopped on the way home to Albuquerque to see my "little old grandmother" as I called her. My mom's mother lived in Colorado, in the same apartment where mom had grown up after her parents divorced. Our grandmother seemed much older than my grandpa, and she really was tiny and frail. She was also very kind. She loved to wrap us up in her arms and listen to our stories. She laughed at our antics. But her apartment was small, and our chaos drove her nuts. So although she looked forward to our visits, and although we enjoyed the attention she gave us, the books she read and the cookies she helped us bake, we didn't ever stay as long as we did when we went to Utah. My grandmother cherished every card or note we ever sent, saving them all, even crayon drawings and school papers. She wrote to us, too, in her beautiful, old-fashioned handwriting.

All of them are now deceased. Just writing about my grandparents makes me aware once again that life is shorter than we think, and that everything we do affects everyone around us. Each of my grandparents loved me out loud. They showed me how much I mattered by what they did with me and for me. They welcomed me into the family without any anxiety about my missing limbs. All three of them thought I was perfect just as I was. They thought that about each of my sisters, and all their other grandchildren, too. Each of us felt we were the favorite.

I think that God intended for human beings to outlive their usefulness in the working world. Everybody needs ordinary, older people whose whole privilege and responsibility is to be good travel companions in life, who know the way, the truth, and the life, and aren't afraid to walk in it. For most of us, that's our grandparents. I'm glad God gave three of them to me.

CHAPTER SIX

Indian and American

As I grew up, mom made sure that I learned about my birth country, India. She expected me to know American geography, too, of course. But she was right that I am not a single-culture person, but one with very deep roots in two quite different ones. My first parents, the first language I ever heard, and the culture that surrounded my babyhood, all dwell across the ocean from the country of my citizenship, and both are important to me.

Mom gave me Indian dolls, Indian children's movies and books, Indian music and newspapers, right along with American Barbie dolls, Walt Disney movies and The Little Engine that Could. She displayed small flags representing each of our birth countries along with the American flag. Jaya and I studied India as part of our home school day, and to-

India Camp, 1995

33

gether we colored maps and pictures of Indian daily life, memorized the names of India's states, and even learned to write a little Hindi. We went to Indian restaurants and tried to make Indian food at home. I still have thick notebooks that Jaya and I compiled, filled with pictures we drew and reports we wrote, articles taken from National Geographic, and material we received from the Indian Embassy on each area of India. It contains glossy brochures from travel agents, along with photographs mom had taken when she traveled to bring us home.

We even had Indian clothing for special occasions. Jaya's was a long, bright pink silk skirt with wide bands of embroidery and a beautiful blouse of the same material. Shanti wore a rich purple-striped silk salwar kameez. The shirt had gold tassels dangling from the hem, and the pants drew tight at the ankle. Mine was simpler, a pale blue cotton with short sleeves and dark blue embroidery. It was definitely a baby dress, because that's what I was. But as Jaya outgrew hers, I inherited it. I realize now those were quite expensive sets of clothing. They were elegantly constructed and embroidered by hand. Mom spent that extra money for a reason. She didn't want us to be ashamed of our country, or to think that everything American was somehow better than what could be found in India. She didn't believe that she had rescued us from an evil place, or a backward one. Her sense was that that she had provided a home for children who needed one, and that the three of us were amazing gifts that India had given to the U.S. and to her. That attitude shaped my perspective, and I have always been grateful for it.

In the summer of 1995, my mom hauled my new red wheelchair on a flat trailer all the way up through the mountains of Colorado so we could attend an Indian culture camp sponsored by WACAP, the American adoption agency through which most of us had been adopted. It was quite exciting to be surrounded by kids that looked pretty much like me, who had all been born in India. It was fascinating for me, Shanti and Jaya to meet other adopted Indian children, as well as Indian men and women living in the U.S. The adults were proud of their roots, and they wanted to help us understand and appreciate the fascinating variety of Indian cultures, customs, arts and music that arose out of the Indian imagination. I loved it all. I liked hearing tales of Indian princesses and stories of Hindu gods. I loved working on Indian art projects, especially since I could use lots of glitter and gold paint. Even trying out Hindi phrases and words from other Indian languages was fun. Although the season was all wrong, we celebrated Holi with brightly colored powder, which we threw energetically on everyone. Every afternoon, each age group practiced dances for the final program. A couple of Indian teenage girls taught us our dance. They had long dark braids and long gold earrings that I didn't have but coveted. The pictures my mom took when we finally performed show me dancing on the floor right in the middle of my class, wearing the hot pink blouse (that had once been Jaya's) with blue shorts. I was laughing out loud. Clearly, I wasn't at all shy or self-conscious in those days! After we danced, mom helped me put on my long pink silk skirt and I paraded around in my new red wheelchair for the rest of the evening, as elegant as Bani Thani, the legendary princess of Rajasthan. I was proud of my dark hair and my brown skin, and proud to be a child of all this beauty. I was only seven, but I remember it as if it were last week.

I was just as enthusiastic when we all put on our red, white and blue shirts and celebrated the Fourth of July with as many fireworks as my mom could amass. She is kind of a fireworks fanatic, and she always looked for a good place outside the city where we could set them off. So we went to every fireworks display she could find. The noise scared me, so she sometimes had to hold me on her lap so she could cover my ears with her hands, but I loved to see the magic explosion of color splashed all over the sky. During the Fourth of July when Rezarta was with us, mom had to work in the hospice unit at Presbyterian Hospital, so she brought us into their large visiting room to watch a fireworks display through the windows, totally noise-free. Now that was really perfect!

We made red, white and blue cupcakes, construction paper flags, and triple-layer trifle with cherry and some kind of blue Jell-O with vanilla pudding. Mom read us the story of America's Declaration of Independence. Together we did many patriotic art projects and watched as many movies as she could find to help us understand the nation that had welcomed us as immigrants, to which we now belonged. She also bought a ten-volume set of children's books called *A History of US* by Joy Hakim. They were so interesting that she read them all aloud to us, book by book, long before I could manage to read them myself. We followed the nation's ups and downs, read through the bad times, the good and the terrific. I happily pledged my allegiance to the flag of the United States of America.

Much later on, I began to think about Jesus and the Kingdom of God. As I learned to read my Bible, I found stories about God's Kingdom, too, and what it looks like in practice. And it dawned on me that although I am proud to be an Indian, India isn't perfect. And although America is a good place to live, and a nation of which I am proud to belong, this country isn't perfect, either. I figured out that no matter where I live, and no matter what country I love, Christians are allowed to be loyal first to God, and to His Kingdom. It's God's perfectly ordinary expectation. Christians pray, "Thy kingdom come," because we know that no country can ever be what God calls His people to be. We are asking for what we have not yet seen. God's Kingdom is upside down and radically different from any political one; a Kingdom where God is joy, justice reigns, peace is practiced, and love is the only law. And that Kingdom is not yet fully present anywhere on earth.

When we obey His command to actually love, to pray and to work for the good of all people, especially our enemies, right there is a little bit of the Kingdom of God we long to see. And that can happen, does happen, all over the world, in every nation, every day. Only those with eyes to see can see it. But God answers prayer, and His Kingdom is coming, God's will is being done, on earth, just as it is in heaven!

It's like a network, a real world wide web of compassion and re-creation. India and America – I am a product of both. I love them both. But both are temporal. I belong to the coming Kingdom of God. My citizenship is there.

CHAPTER SEVEN

On Eagle's Wings

"Once upon a time in a faraway land, there was a girl. She had been given the name Victoria. She grew up in that land with the hills, and was friendly with all the trees and grass. One day Victoria was petting some goats that were eating grass, and she looked up at the blue sky and saw a gold eagle. Her brown eyes shined, and her black hair waved in the air. She got up and looked at the eagle and said, 'What a wonderful, beautiful eagle!'" The sun's great light touched his wings. Victoria's white skin burned red under the sun. She loved the eagle, but he flew by. Victoria ran after the eagle. She ran so fast and so far that she ran to the very end of the world. Then she said goodbye to the eagle and went home. But she lived happily ever after because she saw that beautiful eagle" (Minda Cox, 3rd grade home school writing assignment).

I had already learned to write the same way I draw, with the pencil between my chin and shoulder, but it took me so long that too often I lost my train of thought before I could get my ideas on paper. That's because I use my back and shoulder muscles as well as my little arm to write by "hand." So I got tired pretty fast.

Sometimes when that happened, we just stopped and did something else for a while. An advantage to being schooled at home is that we had freedom to change our schedule or even to abandon it completely, if something interesting came up. In Albuquerque, there was nearly always a festival or other interesting event going on that my mom knew I would like.

I learned how the women at Isleta Pueblo make bread in their outdoor ovens. I took my wheelchair all over Rancho de Las Golondrinas near Santa Fe to discover more about 18th century Spanish colonial life. Together we visited every museum mom could find, several times. Everything was an adventure and made me want to try more, to discover more, and to write about what I learned. I did not feel that my handicap was any particular burden at all. Not having arms or legs was just one single fact about me, not my whole life, and that's exactly how my family treated it.

Looking back, I see how much mom adapted things for me, but then it seemed natural. She was fun, but she was tough, and she never let my disability serve as an excuse not to do my very best. She told me I could accomplish anything I wanted to do, but she also pointed out that wanting to ice skate, for example, was probably a silly ambition. She was both realistic and optimistic. The New Mexico sky shone brilliant blue over my head. I was happy, and life was good.

During the summer after I turned ten, we moved to Memphis. By then I wanted to go to "real" school. But that proved difficult. Most of the city schools weren't accessible at all, and it would have been nearly impossible to make them so. There were stairs everywhere in those beautiful, old buildings. It took weeks of increasingly urgent phone calls to finally get the district to assign me to a school far from our mid-town house. I was happy, because I had a school to attend. However, there was no one at the school who knew anything about how to make a classroom experience actually work for me. The principal had accepted me reluctantly, and couldn't quite imagine what accessibility for a physically disabled but otherwise normal child might mean in practice.

For some reason, he couldn't even acknowledge my need for adapted instruction, insisting that my only issue was being in a wheelchair, which was "no handicap at all" since I was "smart." But my absence of arms and legs did matter. For the first time in my life I became truly dis-abled, and I felt it. If the class was doing a science experiment, my nervous, young teacher made me watch or had me stay at my table and read about it instead of actively participating. When my friends played ball in the gym, the P.E. teacher gave me a red and white plastic beach ball to roll around by myself up on the stage. One afternoon, I slowly and carefully drew a detailed picture of my grandmother, complete with glasses. It wasn't easy to control the pen and my portrait wasn't very good. Still, when I was finished, I was proud. But the only comment written below it reads, "Picture wasn't finished on time." Not long afterwards, I quit drawing altogether.

Music was one of my favorite classes because I loved to sing, but obviously I didn't have fingers to play the recorder we all had to purchase. Some classmate had to stand right behind me and wrap her arms around my body so she could put her own fingers over the holes as I blew. That made me really uncomfortable, and it just seemed stupid and weird. My mom asked why I couldn't just use a xylophone to play the same notes as everyone else, since I could do that myself. The response? "That can't happen. All fourth graders learn to play the recorder." But obviously, I wasn't learning any such thing.

I worked late at night every evening to finish my homework. After a while, mom decided to let me try to use a computer with voice-activated software so that I could do the writing faster. When he heard about it, the principal commented to the accessibility expert that he "wished the parent would allow Minda to use prostheses so she could type on a computer like all the other kids." Clearly, he had no clue. A prosthesis that would reproduce the way wrist, thumb, and four fully-functioning fingers work together to make typing "like all the other kids" possible, does not even exist. I finally got the computer, but when I was in another room learning to use it, I lost points for missing my math class. I felt as if nothing I did was right, or enough.

Even the "handicap" bus that picked me up early every morning turned out to complicate my life. The bus was full of older boys who had behavioral disabilities, plus one little girl with Down's syndrome. It wasn't long before the boys began to taunt my friend and it made me mad. Since she couldn't defend herself, I did. I got in trouble, but I wasn't sorry. Instead of writing the apology that was demanded, I wrote this:

"Today on the bus I fought with this high school boy, Charles. He was calling us "stupid" so I yelled at him. Then he got mad and came back to me. He yelled at me with his fists in my face and I started to cry. The bus driver had to stop the bus. I got in big trouble. But the boys make me mad. They are big and old and mean. I feel like they can be mean to me because I'm little, but when I get mean back or cry because I'm scared, I get in big trouble. I hate to be on that bus. I can't hurt him. I couldn't even get out of my seat. But I get in trouble when he gets up, because they say his handicap is that he can't control his behavior, and I can" (Minda Cox, 4th grade, public school).

I had no idea why being mean was a "handicap." I only knew my friend and I were helpless. There wasn't even an aide on the bus. We were on our own, and that frightened me.

Finally, seeing that I was struggling and desperately unhappy at school, my mom had me tested. She couldn't figure out what was wrong since I had loved learning at home. After noting that my verbal scores were much higher than the performance scores, the test evaluator wrote, "Minda's scores on the performance subtests of the WISC-R are misleading in that three of the four subtests are timed. She was, as a result, penalized for slowness in completing tasks requiring manual problem solving – her scores therefore reflect the effect of her physical handicap on her problem solving skills, rather than those abilities themselves. Her tested IQ falls in the average range of intelligence, but her innate capacity likely falls in the high-average to superior range. "

Of course, I didn't know any of that. All I knew is that I was miserable. I had forgotten the eagle, forgotten the wind, forgotten that I could "run to the very end of the world." The evaluator continued, "Minda is a little girl who has thus far coped remarkably well with some devastating physical limitations. She has invested herself in achieving, and tends to persevere in her efforts. She has also become quite adept in helping others deal with her disability, in that she intentionally engages others in a manner that will put them at ease with her. Unfortunately, the very coping skills that have helped Minda so far tend in her current school to be working against her. In her wish not to "rock the boat" or draw negative attention to herself, Minda is struggling silently with some formidable tasks. She is at a point in her development when mastery and acceptance are the most important issues, and these are the very areas in which she is feeling threatened and undermined. The risk is that she will continue to struggle until she feels defeated, in which case she would lose access to her greatest strengths, which are her intellect and her capacity for engagement."

She was right. I was already feeling defeated. For some reason, instead of helping me bear the not-very-heavy burden of my personal disability, the adults around me seemed to demand that I also bear the much heavier burden of their unwillingness, or inability, to deal with it. And that was simply too much for me to carry or to comprehend. God alone rescued me from that sense of despair for His own purposes. Later that spring, a priest at Grace-St. Luke's Episcopal Church invited people to write a series of Lenten devotions for the forty days before Easter. She asked me to write one using Ezekiel 37:1-14, the prophesy of "dry bones," as my starting place. She knew how I was feeling and thought it would be good for me to read this story for myself. This is what I wrote:

"Sometimes when I am angry I feel as if I were in that valley full of dry bones. I feel as if I were in captivity with Israel. It feels like part of me is dead, and that was what Israel was feeling too. And then I say, 'I will never be glad or free again.' The people of God said that, too. They thought they would never feel alive and that they would never be allowed to go home to Jerusalem ever again. But God was sad, too. So he said, 'I can bring you joy and gladness.' Then he took them home. That's what he says to me in my heart: 'I can bring you joy and gladness.' Then he does. He makes me feel alive again, and he takes me home. My home is God."

It was true. It still is. To God, I have never been a problem. I am just "Minda." I am an ordinary person. With God, I am always "at home." What Virginia Brown, both priest and friend, printed below the devotion is equally revealing:

"Minda says of herself, 'I am ten years old and I would like to forget about school. But when I grow up I want to write true stories. And my words will fly on the wings of my heart.'"

Clearly I was discouraged, but also not defeated. I was still willing to wait, and the "beautiful eagle" of my favorite story was still calling

41

to me. Only long afterwards did I read Isaiah 40:31, now so close to my heart: "Those who wait for the Lord will renew their strength, they shall mount up with wings like eagles, they shall run and not be weary, they shall walk and not faint."

What I began to learn, and what I am still learning, is that it is always right to wait for God. It is the most ordinary thing in the world to do, and also one of the hardest. Only waiting for Him makes it easy, even for those of us with no legs, to run the race that is set before us.

CHAPTER EIGHT

I-CAN. I Can't

In the summer of 1999, mom got a phone call from someone who would quickly become one of her best friends. Susan Easley and her husband, Brett, have a house full of both adopted and birth children, some of them disabled in various ways. We had moved to Memphis so that mom could buy a house in mid-town, across the street from Grace-St. Luke's Episcopal Church. It was a wonderful, old house with a huge front porch, and served as a gathering place for Rivendell Community members and many others.

Susan saw an article about "intentional" Christian communities in the area, including the Rivendell Community, and picked up the phone. She said, "I saw the picture and a write-up in the Memphis newspaper. It was beautiful – light streaming in the window, Cathy touching Minda's face gently, and Minda with her long, beautiful hair sitting in a wheelchair. I knew I had to meet them.

It was a delight to become acquainted with their family and their community. The hours spent around the feet of the storyteller, the dangerous driving escapades that our two 'wheelchair girls' engaged in (that we only learned about later!), and the gentle cadence of life at Rivendell, were to be the subject of memories for the rest of our lives. There was a joy present in Cathy and Minda's life that was jarring in its way, because the depth was unexpected. There was music, laughter, cooking and baking. With no notice, visitors would drop by and join in. They would share their triumphs and seek answers for their problems. No one was turned away and I don't remember anyone leaving empty-handed. Books and baked goods were shared freely, with no expectation of reciprocity. Yet the return on their investment always seemed exponential.

It was a precious time, and we were content. It was what I wanted for all of my children, but especially those born differently-abled. I wanted them to be comfortable with themselves, the world around them, and to better understand the Author and Finisher of their lives."

Pretty quickly, Susan introduced us to an organization for children with limb differences called I-CAN (International Child Amputee Network) and invited mom and me to go with her and her children to Atlanta for the annual summer gathering. It was the perfect antidote to a hard school year, and I was eager to go.

If I had thought it was cool to be among a bunch of East Indians at culture camp (and I did) this was even more amazing. Everywhere I looked there were children, teens and adults with some kind of limb loss. Most of them were missing a hand or a leg, or like Susan's daughter Abbi, both arms. But this was hardly the time to compare missing body parts to see whose disability topped someone else's. If you are able-bodied, perhaps you can't quite wrap your mind around how at home we felt when everyone we saw stood out, either for their own visible disability, or because they were family members of someone who was "the same different as me," to use a line from a recent book title. Whenever we went out to eat or to the hotel's pool, people stared at all of us. For the first time in my life, I felt almost anonymous! In fact, I noticed that in a restaurant, more people stared at kids like Abbi, who can eat anything with her feet and does it flawlessly, than at me. It was a weird reversal. I found a whole bunch of kids who were totally ordinary yet disabled, and who knew exactly what it was like to be seen all the time. That was freeing and fun.

But I also noticed that a few of them were hiding their little arm, or covering up a prosthetic leg. It was the first time that I'd ever felt totally normal and ordinary in a crowd, but it was also the first time I'd ever met children who were ashamed, or afraid of their differences. It seemed strange to me. I just didn't get it. Different is just different. It isn't anything else, certainly not a reason for shame.

Susan and my mom were instant friends because they are both Christians, both had adopted disabled children, and both free to do whatever they think makes sense, without worrying too much about other people's opinions. They think so much alike, they share the same wicked sense of humor, and they love each other's company. I do, too, and it was a good thing that I'd already learned to enjoy adventures, because whenever I went anywhere with the Easley's, something unusual was likely to happen. And it was always hilarious.

"Several of our children came from orphanages. Early on, I got in the habit of taking all of the children with me, nearly every time I went out. When Minda visited, there was no exception. She would be swept up into The Eggplant (our 15-passenger Dodge Van) along with everyone else.

The thing I'll always remember most about Minda is her sense of humor. One time I noticed she was being stared at by a man in a not-so-kindly way. We were stuck in the long check-out line at Wal-Mart, and it was hard to ignore what looked like annoyance in his face, as if he were upset that we had ruined his perfectly good day just by being there. I crouched down so I was at 'Minda-level' and we both looked straight at the guy. I smiled and winked, and Minda waved her stump. Apparently he hadn't thought we knew what he was doing. He quickly turned away frustrated, shaking his head, uncomfortable. Minda said, loudly enough to be over heard, 'He SHOULD feel guilty, look at all those limbs he's hogging for himself. Didn't his mother ever teach him to share?!'"

I said it, but Susan egged me on! Nothing embarrassed Susan, not even herding around a dozen noisy children, many of us disabled. Now I know that it is controversial even to use the word disabled. Differently-abled is more politically correct, and in many ways it is also more true. Like my mom, Susan didn't cut us any slack. If we wanted to go somewhere, we had to get ready, do chores and be ready on time. She held no pity-parties at her house. And that was such a delicious thing, to be expected by someone other than my mom to just get on with life, knowing that I could. There are an astonishing number of things that people do not expect me to accomplish, that I manage very well. I am grateful for the abilities God has given me, and for persistence to find ways to get things done.

But the other side of this coin is that many of us who are missing multiple limbs, or in wheelchairs because of arthrogryposis or spina bifida, actually can't do everything. There are things that are simply impossible for me to do without help. There are many things I cannot manage, even with assistance.

There is such a negative cultural assumption about people with disabilities, even today, that sometimes I have tried really hard to pretend that I can do everything everyone else can do. Sometimes I have dishonored the truth by covering up my struggles. Neither my mom, nor Susan, ever encouraged that. Pride alone speaks that language.

No problems? That's just not real. All ordinary people struggle. Disabled ones do, too.

Joni Erickson Tada is one of my heroines because she does not pretend anything. I have heard her on the radio saying something like, "I wake up every day hating my paralysis. And then I have to decide whether to praise God or to remain in that dark place." She can't scratch her nose if it itches, or turn over by herself, or take a book off the shelf. She is also an accomplished artist, author and speaker. She is disabled. She is differently-abled. She is competent. She is handicapped. And she is also both honest and full of joy. That is what I want to be.

I have been extremely frustrated sometimes and angry with my limitations. Often I'm just plain tired of struggling to get done all the ordinary things that life demands. What helps me then is turning to Jesus who says, "Come to me all you who are weary and are carrying heavy burdens, and I will give you rest. Take my yoke upon you and learn from me; for I am gentle and humble in heart, and you will find rest for your souls. For my yoke is easy, and my burden is light" (Matthew 11:28-29).

When I carry this burden myself, it is too heavy. And often enough I become discouraged. Not everyone sees that, because I do not think it helps anybody to hear me complain. But I want to be honest, too, and write the whole truth—to live without arms or legs is a heavy burden, and carrying it wears me out. But as soon as I take Jesus' yoke and learn from Him again how to rest, and to trust, I realize that He truly does take the weight; His yoke is easy, and His burden is light. It is the truth. But it is a truth I have to learn over and over and over. God gives me rest. I do not just grab it, and then sit down to possess peace and joy as if they were mine to control. It is always God.

So, you want to know what I cannot do?

I cannot lift a suitcase and take it out to the car.

I can't put on my own underwear or swimming suit.

I can't take my crock pot down off the counter.

If it is raining hard, I can't "walk" to school; I did it once in a Memphis rainstorm and ended up stranded in the middle of the street with a dead wheelchair. When the roads or sidewalks are full of snow, I cannot just step through the drifts or climb over them to make my way to class. I can't ice skate, roller skate, climb a tree, take a hike up a mountain, swim across the pool, ride a bike or run a marathon. I can't hold a glass over the sink and turn on the faucet at the same time.

I can't turn a key in the lock, get inside a room if the door opens outward, or play a recorder.

I can't even open a new tube of watercolor. I can't run up the steps with my friends to a second floor classroom.

I can't scratch a mosquito bite.

I can't. I often wish I could. And that is why what I can do matters so much. I can refuse bitterness. I can follow Jesus. I can be faithful to whatever He asks me to do. I can "come to Him" again and again, lose the burden, and find rest. And I can take Paul seriously, he who loved the Lord Jesus, and called his handicap a "gift."

"I was given the gift of a handicap to keep me in constant touch with my limitations. Satan's angel did his best to get me down; what he in fact did was push me to my knees. At first I didn't think of it as a gift, and begged God to remove it. Three times I did that, and then he told me, My grace is enough; it's all you need. My strength comes into its own in your weakness. Once I heard that, I was glad to let it happen. I quit focusing on the handicap and began appreciating the gift. It was a case of Christ's strength moving in on my weakness..." (2 Cor. 12:9-10, The Message).

It is the truth. And that is why my life, like yours, is ordinary. There's nothing special about any of us. Rather, we are all unique creations, each of us "special." And if we are wise, we learn to turn our eyes away from ourselves and our problems and onto Jesus. And then, onto the people who need the gifts He has given us to offer.

I-CAN. I can't. God does…more than we can ask or expect!

CHAPTER NINE

More Gifts

Adolescence. Oh, help. What do I say about those years? Every teenager in America suffers in one way or another. So did I. I was increasingly self-conscious, for one thing. I just knew that everyone was looking at me all the time. Unfortunately, that feeling didn't reflect only teenage angst; it was the simple truth. To just be able to disappear in a crowd of my peers became my whole heart's desire.

We had moved again, this time to Missouri in 2000, where my mom and a couple of our friends wanted to extend the ministry of Rivendell, the intentional Christian community they had started in Memphis. Right away they turned an enclosed porch at the back of our new house into a convenient, accessible classroom with space for me to be by myself to read, write or daydream. Light poured in through the east windows and played on my long, low desk made from a door. I could spread things out to my heart's content. I loved it! Nobody minded if I spent an afternoon totally by myself. That's where I could rest from the public eye and gather strength to go back out again, to smile and speak to strangers who stared, to be on display, to be exhibit A, the friendly, handicapped kid who didn't want to make anyone uncomfortable.

But I was also twelve, longing for some social independence that was hard to achieve. "Walking" with a heavy electric wheelchair made it flat impossible to jump into a friend's car and take off for the mall on a Saturday afternoon. Even if someone volunteered to take my manual chair along, shopping wasn't much fun for my friend, because her hands were already full, just pushing me around. It wasn't fun for me either, because I couldn't reach things I liked, nothing fit me right, and I couldn't try on clothes by myself, anyway.

It was stressful for me and not easy for my mom to have to come along to every event just because no one else knew how to manage my chair or had a vehicle that could accommodate it. I couldn't even get in to most people's houses. And once inside, there wasn't room to navigate my wheelchair. Should I just get down and "walk" on the floor? What if I had to use the bathroom when I was away from home?

When I sang in the church youth choir, an adult had to lift me up from my wheelchair and carry me to my place in the sanctuary, since there was no room for a wheelchair and no ramp like we had in Memphis. When the others processed out after church, I sat in the choir stall and waited to be lifted down again. Everything became a big deal in those years, hard for me and hard for everyone else. Looking back, nobody would say it was easy.

So a couple of years later, when the Community bought an Amish house to convert into a retreat center on many acres of land near Bolivar, leaving Springfield did not distress me at all. Quiet surrounded me, as well as huge stars, peace and beauty. I continued to study at home, but I could take long walks in my electric wheelchair, and watch the turkey buzzards soar over our land. I could sit on the big porch and listen to the spring peepers down by the pond, hear our Amish neighbors singing in the evening, and enjoy Saturday night suppers with whatever interesting guests came for retreats.

My mom was ordained as a priest in the Episcopal Church during the fall of 2003, and began working at St. Alban's, a small congregation of amazing people who worship in a beautiful building on the edge of Bolivar. She loved it immediately. Bolivar is the town of her dreams, I think! Raised on the prairie in South Dakota where her heart has always longed to return, she took to rural Missouri immediately. Even ten years later, she still walks around saying things like, "I love Bolivar!" It's true. She also loves having a university practically next door.

Next to God and other people, my mom loves school: any school. She loved the Nazarene Seminary in Kansas City, where she graduated before I was born. She loved Regis College, the Jesuit school in Denver, where she began her university studies. She loved teaching in New Mexico. Books and people and God—that is my mom. So she started haunting the Southwest Baptist University library, taking me to SBU concerts and plays, and hanging out in the bookstore.

St. Alban's has been really blessed to have Dr. Kathy Brown as our organist for nearly twenty years. She teaches voice all week at SBU, and then comes to play wonderful music for us. Of course, mom and Kathy became friends right away. During September, as we began our home school classes, mom asked her if she knew anyone who might be able to teach me art. For years I had wanted to try again, but was a little afraid and didn't know how to begin. Now that we were near a university, she thought maybe there was a student who might help me get started.

Kathy did better than that. She contacted her friend, Emily, the wife of Dr. Jim Frost, who directs the Intercultural Studies program at SBU. Emily is an extraordinary artist, and she agreed to meet me at St. Alban's.

"Are you Minda?" I wheeled around to see a smiling woman with shining blue eyes. "Yes," I replied. And that is all it took. I felt as if I had known her forever. There was never any sense of strangeness, and not a single glance that betrayed her uneasiness with my disability. It was almost as if she didn't even notice.

I found out just how true that was when she began teaching me! She asked if I was serious about being an artist. And as soon as I said yes, my limitations faded out of the picture altogether. She was bound and determined that I could do anything she assigned, and since she was working hard to teach me to see and to draw, she didn't expect any less than hard work from me.

My first efforts were hopeless. But Emily was convinced that I was not. She pushed and prodded and figured out ways to work around my disability without sacrificing excellence. Actually, that was one of her favorite words – excellence. She gave it. She expected it. And I tried to give it back, too.

Eventually, my mom quit even trying to teach me anything else. We put away all my other textbooks and I spent every day and half the evening drawing, reading books on art, figuring out perspective and trying to draw both accurately and creatively. She figured that serious study of art involved all those other subjects, anyway. It was hard work, and I loved it all.

Not long after I started art lessons with Emily, Kathy made a surprising request. Another friend, Dana Hacker, taught a class in Child Development at SBU. She had previously invited parents of disabled children to come and speak to her class when they studied Exceptional Children, and she'd found that to be a good learning experience for the students.

Later, Dana wrote, "I often wished we could also hear from the mouths of the children involved, but I was afraid they were too fragile for the experience…UNTIL I met Minda! My friend and colleague, Kathy Brown, had suggested a young teen from the church where she plays organ. She assured me that Minda was loaded with confidence. Still, I hesitated to put someone in the spot of addressing sometimes brash college students, especially a teenager arriving in a motorized wheelchair.

Minda rolled in (literally) on that first day of class, beaming with personality. I remember that her mom interacted with the students, and Minda joined in occasionally. Later, Minda whispered to me that she could handle it by herself 'next time.' From that moment on, I had my students' favorite guest speaker each semester on call. Often at the end of the semester, student evaluations reflected how much Minda's talk meant to them, and the words 'life changing' were often used. I felt the same way. I learned from her each time, and was inspired by her courage and confidence. Her strong mother bowed out to allow her daughter to express herself freely…"

That wasn't the whole story. I liked telling stories of my family and childhood, I wasn't shy about my disability, and I enjoyed the students. It was fun to be on campus. I loved it, actually, because everywhere I went, people were friendly. But I didn't imagine that I'd ever be a student at SBU. I wasn't that confident! University attendance was absolutely out of the question for me. I knew I had trouble with math, couldn't possibly keep up with lab classes, and besides, everything else I did took me three times longer than it took any of the students who were listening to me in Dana's classes.

Still, I kept going back semester after semester, finding myself more and more comfortable speaking about my life, my dreams, and my experience growing up different. It was good for me to hear myself tell those stories and to see that it mattered to others to hear them. Sometimes, listening to students give their oral reports before I spoke, I even dared to think, "I could do that about as well as they are!" Art was a gift. Learning to speak to others was another gift. God's people were particular gifts to me. Even my shy nature turned out to be a gift. I was full to the brim!

Emily mentioned college occasionally, Dana did, and even Kathy asked me about taking classes when I completed my home school years. But I just couldn't imagine myself doing it. My art made me happy, and I felt confident and competent as I drew and painted. I even tried my hand at linocut!

Besides, when I went by myself to talk with Dana's students, I had to wait outside for someone to come along and open the door into her building. I couldn't find any accessible bathrooms. There were elevators in only some of the buildings. How would I sit at a desk, anyway? How could I carry a tray in the cafeteria? How would I ever take notes fast enough to keep up in a classroom full of normal college students? And how on earth would I pay for it? No. SBU was not for me. But, secretly, I wished it could be.

CHAPTER TEN

Following the Leaders

I started attending the Episcopal Church Women's conferences when I was twelve or thirteen, because my mom always went and it was easier to take me along than to leave me home. That's how I began to develop strong relationships with some great women four or five times my age. I hadn't ever heard the word mentor, but in many ways that's what they became for me. They also treated me like one of them, not like a child.

Since my mom had her own friends, she usually abandoned me as soon as we got into the room and left me to make mine. It was never difficult. Women generally enjoy talking to each other, and that I could do. It was invaluable to see inside the hearts and minds of these Episcopal women, including retired professors, ordained clergy, women with responsible careers, and some very ordinary women like me. I learned a lot just by hanging out with them, hearing them question each other, challenge each other, tell stories of their lives, and laugh together. It was good for me to see that my outspoken mother wasn't the only strong woman in the world, and to watch her across the room having the time of her life deep in probably controversial conversation with other women who loved God and loved the church.

I imagine those early friendships gave me confidence to speak to Dana's students later on. They also made me eager to participate even more broadly with adults in the church, even though I was still very young. My mom reminded me that adolescence is temporary, adulthood is forever. If I couldn't easily do teenage activities with friends my age, then I might as well do adult ones. That actually made sense to me.

So I attended Episcopal Church conventions every fall with crowds of adults, participated in adult Sunday School, and enjoyed other adult educational and service opportunities. For me, those times were anything but boring. I was used to studying on my own, and seeking out information I wanted to learn. I discovered that adult conversation was interesting, even when it went way over my head. One of the clergy leaders, a great friend whose spiritual and social wisdom I tried to follow, remembers my adolescence this way:

"A number of years ago when Minda was in her early teen years, I served as the coordinator of education for lay persons in the Episcopal Diocese of West Missouri. Over a four-year period, clergy, university and seminary professors offered day-long seminars four to six times a year on Church and faith related topics including theology, church history, liturgy, the sacraments, Episcopal Church polity, and what it meant to express one's faith in daily life. The seminars were scholarly and challenging, designed for adult learners. But Minda participated in each and every seminar. But not only was she present, she was highly participatory. Never intimidated by a scholarly presenter or an adult audience, Minda asked questions, raised issues, and always offered valuable contributions to the discussions. Even as a young teen, Minda was serious about growing in her knowledge and love of God, eager to grow closer to God not only with her heart, but with her mind" (the Rev. Susan McCann).

It's funny to read that now. Susan was right, I did love it. I was interested. People and their ideas do fascinate me. But I was ignorant compared to the men and women huddled around those large round tables. I had none of their life experience. It didn't scare me to feel kind of dumb, and for sure I didn't feel unwelcome, but I wouldn't have said I was especially precocious, either. There was a lot I didn't know. I was only a teenager eager to understand, that's all.

There was much to learn, and I didn't find it easy. Since I was always present, I did complete the whole program, which not very many of the adults actually did. Only looking back do I understand how valu-

55

able that was – to learn to just keep on keeping on. Only now do I see that my mind absorbed far more than I realized at the time – information, yes, but also a conviction about my freedom and responsibility under God to think, to learn and to discover the goodness of the Lord for myself.

So many of the strong women I got to know then remain my friends today. When I found my way to SBU and needed money to help with tuition, it was the Episcopal Church Women who found scholarship money for me every year. And they asked me to speak to their gatherings, to show my art, and to tell them about my hopes and dreams.

If I tried to name them all, this paragraph alone would stretch to several pages. But I do need to mention one more, Mary Howe. During these years, the Rt. Rev. Barry Howe was the Episcopal Bishop of west Missouri. I know the word bishop conjures up all kinds of mental images for evangelical Protestants, many of them negative. It wasn't easy, once I got to SBU, to explain to Baptists why we Episcopalians even have them. But Barry Howe doesn't fit any negative stereotype. He's got a wonderful sense of what matters, and what does not, for one thing. Mostly, he's a vibrant, gentle Christian. He was a great bishop, with a perfectly delightful wife.

We don't have thrones for our bishops, although there may be a few bishops who wish we did, but everyone agreed that Mary was really the power behind Barry's folding chair. Power might be the wrong word. She was perhaps the joy behind it; the glad presence that sustained him as he dealt with ecclesiastical crises and everyday problems so calmly.

Mary laughs all the time, and she knows everyone's name. If that sounds like a silly thing to mention, try to remember how much it has sometimes mattered to you when someone looked at you with full attention and affection, and called you by name. That's what Mary did. She knew everyone, and cared about everyone. She cared about me, too. She held all our concerns in her heart, and everyone knew it. Her memory for faces, names, and concerns is remarkable.

She is smart and funny and wise, but mostly, she's exquisitely able to make everyone feel, and to actually be, at home in her presence, which is also God's. That kind of hospitality of heart isn't as common among Christians as it ought to be. I am still learning to practice it. But I've learned from watching Mary interact with all sort of people in many different circumstances, that nothing matters as much for building and demonstrating Christian community as beautiful, ordinary hospitality does. Slowly, slowly, I think I'm becoming what I saw in those women.

"I've had the privilege of knowing Minda for a very long time so there are many stories I could share about the remarkable little girl who is now an extraordinary young woman. What I most want to express is that Minda lives and moves and has her being happily centered in God. Her life is lived in unwavering faith in the never-failing love and goodness of our Lord, and that faith is expressed in joy, in gratitude, and in service to others" (the Rev. Susan McCann).

There is nothing I would rather hear than that. If it is true at all, it is because I have tried to put my wheels where some ordinary, godly women first put their feet.

CHAPTER ELEVEN

Camp Barnabas

When summer came to Missouri, the fliers for church camp appeared, tacked onto the bulletin board. Of course, mom signed us all up. For a couple of years, camp was terrific for me, for Shanti, and for Jaya, too. But then, the camp director changed. Suddenly, the counselors who had taken me in the canoe before couldn't let me go on the float trip because "we can't guarantee your safety." Of course, they couldn't actually guarantee anybody's safety, and anyway, I float! When I go overboard, there's nothing to drag me down. I just bob along on the surface until someone grabs me up again. And, obviously, I wear a safety vest like everyone else. But no, it was "wait inside and watch a movie."

I didn't react to that very well, I'm afraid. It was just another one of those absurd situations that made no sense to me, that seemed unreasonable and unfair, and there wasn't anything I could do about it. It is right to protect kids from excessive danger, but it seemed to me that in this case, as in so many others, adults were generally more interested in protecting themselves from risk, by limiting what I was allowed to do, than in protecting me from any actual harm.

It isn't disability itself that holds people back, but what others think the disability means. I was lucky in that my mom didn't think it meant much of anything, and her attitude was a counter-weight to other messages I heard. But still, knowing that she thought I should be allowed to do things, and that she encouraged me to, didn't keep me from resenting it when safety became more important than adventure.

When I heard about Camp Barnabas, a real camp designed specifically for disabled kids, I wanted to go see it immediately. Mom and our Rivendell friend, Susie Danielsson, drove me down to Purdy, Missouri to see if the camp measured up to the hype. The reality far surpassed what we expected. Oh, it was primitive, all right. In those days, before Extreme Home Makeover arrived on the scene, all the cabins were too small for the wheelchairs that had to be crammed into the space. There wasn't any air conditioning, despite the sticky July heat. The bathrooms weren't even close to the cabins, but there was laughter! I saw a couple hundred disabled kids doing everything you can imagine, including swimming, horseback riding, singing ridiculous songs, hiking and laughing. It was real camp. It was definitely normal, but the campers were not, at least by other people's standards. Camp Barnabas represented sanity, the rich and fruitful ordinary that human life is supposed to be. So who was behind all this wonderful craziness? It didn't take me long to find out. Paul and Cyndy Teas were Camp Barnabas, its heart and soul, its life.

Cyndy Teas had once been the director of nurses at Camp Kanakuk, a Christian sports camp in southern Missouri. Years before I met her, she had tried to support one of their regular campers who returned to Kanakuk the summer after losing her leg to sarcoma. The girl was glad to be back, but discouraged, tired, and frustrated because there were suddenly so many things she couldn't do. Camp Barnabas came to birth, at least in Cyndy's mind, as she talked to that teenager who wanted to go to a camp "where she felt normal." Cyndy's instinctive response was, "We have to re-create normal." With no money, and a whole lot of faith in the God who gives us vision, courage, and enthusiasm, Paul and Cyndy began planning and looking for land. The whole story is told in the book Camp Barnabas by Heno Head. It's a great story. They are great people who know they serve a great God.

By the summer of 2004, when I first attended the camp session for physically disabled teens, the Teas' house at camp was falling down, although you'd never have guessed it if you didn't already know. They never talked about their needs. Camp Barnabas didn't turn anybody away, even if the child's family couldn't afford the fees. But somehow, the camp's huge bills for food and electricity and salaries always got paid, even if the Teas' themselves did not. They knew every camper by name from the first time that a new mom or dad drove through the gate. Everyone was enthusiastically greeted by Paul, who stayed at the entrance of Barnabas until the last car with the last camper was inside. It made for a long, hot day but he seemed to love it. Everyone, not only campers, but parents and siblings, were drawn into the circle of his easy affection. To tell the truth, I wasn't sure how much of that I wanted.

"I remember the first time Minda arrived at camp," Cyndy wrote. "I opened her car door, and told her I would help her out so she wouldn't fall. The car was parked on a slight hill and I was afraid she would slip getting down into her wheelchair. Minda snapped, 'I don't need any help!' She was right, of course. She got out just fine. But it was at that moment that I knew I liked this independent Minda, and also that God had plans for us to be friends. I suspected that He would use each of us to help the other grow."

I loved camp that summer – the horses, the canoes, the crowded cabins, even archery. Having the same college girl to assist me with personal care for the whole week made it easier to ask for help. Camp Barnabas is unique that way, by providing a single volunteer counselor for each camper for the whole week called CIAs (Christians In Action).

But it wasn't all sweetness and light. Awkward and bossy, I knew I needed some assistance, yet I also didn't want any more than I really required. I had no idea how to teach someone else how to help me with bathing or toileting, without being both embarrassed and demanding. I was nervous anyway, being needy in such personal things. I didn't know how the counselors saw me or what they thought of my body. Here were beautiful, strong young women just a few years older than me having to help me to the bathroom. It was difficult not to express jealousy at their easy grace. I was self-conscious, of course, but I was also rude. I knew it, but I couldn't seem to relax. Being a Christian didn't erase teen angst, for sure! But it did make me aware that I needed more of God's wisdom than I had, and more of His courtesy towards others.

My mom knew what I could do easily and what was hard for me. We had done all my personal care together for so long that it was instinctive for us both. The counselors didn't know how best to help me, they were young, and as embarrassed as I was trying to get everything right. They needed encouragement as much as I did, but I didn't know how to give it to them. Sometimes I hesitated to express myself until I was really upset, which didn't help either. I was abrupt, especially when I wanted so much for one of them to accept me as an equal, and she wanted to see me as the needy one she had been assigned to assist. We had to adjust to each other and that wasn't always smooth.

Over the next couple of summers, Cyndy sought me out a few times each session just to talk. I took myself to her, too, when I was especially discouraged. Cyndy wrote, "It was great to meet Minda first as a teen, when her whole job was to act independent, and to be 'selfish.' Minda reacted because other young people assumed she couldn't do anything for herself, just because of her missing arms and legs. She felt they treated her like a baby. Sometimes they did, too. But when Minda came to me to complain about her counselor, she also listened when I gave her counsel and urged her to be more patient. Of course, she filtered everything through the mind of an ordinary sixteen-year-old, but nevertheless, she learned, she grew, and she allowed God to change her little by little. To see her now as a young adult woman is a great joy. All her teenage hurt and anger has dissolved and been replaced by a true servant's heart."

I did listen. I knew it was my own need to control everything that got in my way. I recognized the down-side of my independence and perfectionism. But I didn't know how to change that in myself, or even how to understand it. Cyndy had wisdom to offer. She told me about her own struggles growing up, reassuring me that what I was experiencing was pretty common to all teenagers struggling into adulthood. I know she and Paul prayed for me, and they prayed with me, too. I had needed that circle of easy affection more than I knew. From the beginning, Paul has been a kind of "dad" to me, strong and gentle and full of God. And Cyndy quickly became another in the string of moms I had been urged to collect!

That is how they treated everyone. I was only one of hundreds of disabled campers, parents and siblings, as well as staff and volunteers who discovered, and then became part of, the Barnabas family. As I matured, grew in my art, and became more patient with myself and with other people, my world expanded. A lot of it began at Camp Barnabas.

Paul and Cyndy urged me to take risks in ways that were hard for me then, to dare to make friends with other young adults who were not disabled, or who were disabled in ways I was not. They taught me to see those girls for who they were – ordinary fellow-Christians, anxious to please, awkward themselves, and unsure about how to relate to me. So slowly I began to notice their need for my assurance and compassion. I began to let my counselors see who I was on the inside. I tried to show them how to pay less attention to my obvious differences, and more to what we had in common. It became easier to tell the truth about my struggles, and even to tell the truth about my dreams for my future. I began to talk to them as equals, without being so defensive, but also without hiding my determination and passion. I learned not to demand that every nervous new volunteer (who had never even seen anyone like me before) do whatever I needed done in exactly the way I was used to having it done. I felt that they began to see me less as a "handicapped girl" and more like what I knew myself to be an ordinary girl who happens not to have arms or legs. As others began to recognize how run-of-the-mill ordinary I really am, God began to show me my uniqueness in some new ways.

Emily had urged me to put people into my paintings for a long time, but I was stuck on landscapes, flowers and trees, which I insisted that I preferred, partly because I was too afraid to try to paint human beings. I just absolutely knew I couldn't do that. I couldn't even look at my own body to understand how hands move, or how an ankle crosses the other, since I just didn't have those parts. I really had no idea how it felt to run, or to get down on my knees, or to clench a fist. That made it hard to draw those actions. But mostly, I was afraid to fail. I could do an exercise on drawing hair with my ebony pencil if Emily assigned it, or lips, or an ear all carefully shaded and correct. But when I looked at a real person and needed to draw her with pencil on paper, I froze. I made excuses, not very good ones, and I procrastinated. And sometimes I just got mad.

After I gathered up the nerve to ask the Barnabas staff to figure out some way to strap me into a harness so that I could fly down the long (and high!) zip line, my perspective on what is possible changed almost immediately. As they always did when faced with a challenge, the guys rigged up something to make the harness secure for me, because they always said that any camper could do anything. I believed them, and I wanted to try. But to tell the truth, at the last minute I was scared to death! Sometimes that streak of stubbornness helps me out in a crisis – I wasn't about to let them think I was afraid!

Once I was released, and out there on my own, I felt something I had never felt before. Racing through the air and speeding down towards earth was an amazing experience. I was helpless, and yet secure. I didn't have any control at all, but I knew I was safe. Barely on the ground, I wanted to do it all over again. No matter how often I did it, the zipline never got old to me. It was a special gift to enjoy that sense of wild freedom from my normal physical limitations.

Then, something shifted in my perspective. I had fallen and been caught; I'd been dropped off a high platform and saved; I'd flung myself outside my control zone and found God laughing with me all the way down. It was exhilarating! After that experience, I came home and began to draw and paint what I really loved most of all and hadn't dared to draw – people.

The camp was named for Barnabas, a Jesus-follower, whose story is told in the New Testament (Acts 9:26-28). When Paul first became a believer, no one trusted him. None of the disciples wanted anything to do with the man who had so bitterly, and so successfully, persecuted the Church. It was Barnabas who risked his own reputation when he took Paul to the other disciples and interceded for him. He is the one who told the others what great things God had done for Paul. Barnabas welcomed Paul when no one else did, because he believed what Paul said about himself and his experience with the risen Lord. Bar-nabas – Son of Encouragement.

Paul and Cyndy Teas chose that name to indicate that their camp would encourage anyone who walked, wheeled, or was carried in. They would love the campers outrageously, but they would also pour their own Christian faith and courage into each one, giving strength and encouraging campers, volunteers and staff to reach way beyond their limitations. They did that for me.

Barnabas did it, too. He gave Paul cheerful friendship and hope, despite the odds that were stacked against him in Jerusalem. But Barnabas' encouragement also meant that he tried to soften a few of Paul's more obvious rough edges before meeting with those understandably suspicious Christians. His wise counsel probably included urging Paul to listen before he spoke, and to give the other fellows a chance to get to know his heart.

Lots of God's people go around prickly and self-protective, not just Paul, and not just those of us who are disabled. Everybody needs true encouragement from friends who will help knock the chips off our shoulders, so we can more freely run the race that is set before us.

CHAPTER TWELVE

Becoming an Artist

A t the end of my sophomore year, Emily wrote an evaluation of our class, in which she mentioned the books we had used. When I look back now, I am astounded. We had worked through much of Art Fundamentals: Theory and Practice by Ocvirk, Bone, Stinson and Wigg; Drawing: You Can Do It by Greg Albert; Watercolor Techniques by Tony Couch; Drawing Nature by Stanley Maltzman; Exploring Color by Nita Leland; and several others as well. We had covered the principles of organization, elements of art, color, design and composition, as well as drawing and watercolor painting techniques. My notebook for that first year is several inches think, full of the handouts and assignments she gave me.

Emily expected a lot. Because I loved what I was learning, and because she was so encouraging and enthusiastic, I did my best to meet her expectations. The truth is I was perfectly content to do nothing else. She noted that I "obviously spent hours" on my work. That sentence reflected the reality. My whole room was designed for me to work all day, alternating between drawing at one table and painting in a separate space. With no need to put things away out of sight, the different pads of paper, all my drawing pencils and brushes, and the palettes of beautiful watercolors, were always ready for me, inviting me to come right into the world of art and be at home.

Sometimes I felt overwhelmed. I am not naturally a quick reader, or a quick learner, either. I like to take time to understand something before I do it. I have to think before I speak. I felt pressured to keep up

65

with her long assignments, and anxious that if I didn't do well, she'd give up and quit teaching me. It was easy to get disgusted with myself, too, because I couldn't easily translate what I wanted to express into an actual drawing. She tried to teach me that my brain, eye and little arm had to learn how to work together, and that this would take time. My own impatience, mixed with an eagerness to please her, made it harder for me to enter the process, which inevitably included more failures than successes. I was ashamed of every mistake and tried to make excuses for every failure. I found it difficult to expose myself to her necessary criticism, no matter how helpful it was, or how gently given. I kept at it though, and she did, too.

At the end of that first year, Emily wrote, "I was very pleased with Minda's obvious gifts in drawing and painting. Any lack of confidence, I believe, was due to the amount of work I expected from her, and her propensity toward perfectionism. In fact, I have been so impressed with Minda that at times I would forget she had a disability at all and go right ahead and give her assignments that an average student would balk at for certain."

Emily also wrote, "Sometimes she would call me for help, out of fear that she might not do the lesson 'perfectly.' It has taken a while for her to realize that most of her present work is part of the process of learning, not for showing to others. I try to get her to be easy on herself. I stress over and over again to ENJOY THE PROCESS. At the same time, we can use this bent toward perfectionism to advantage. The more she relaxes, though, the better her drawing will become. We will address this issue more closely next semester."

That summer I went to Camp Barnabas for the first time and dared the zipline that changed everything, even my art. My efforts to portray people began to lead to more polished drawing and paintings. Some of them were beautiful. I was still shy about saying that then, but I was beginning to see a future, one in which art played a big part. I was beginning to identify myself as an artist.

Still, it is probably only slowly that most of us cautious ones lose fear and plunge ahead into God's future. Emily once asked me to name what I saw as my biggest roadblock to just enjoying watercolor, which

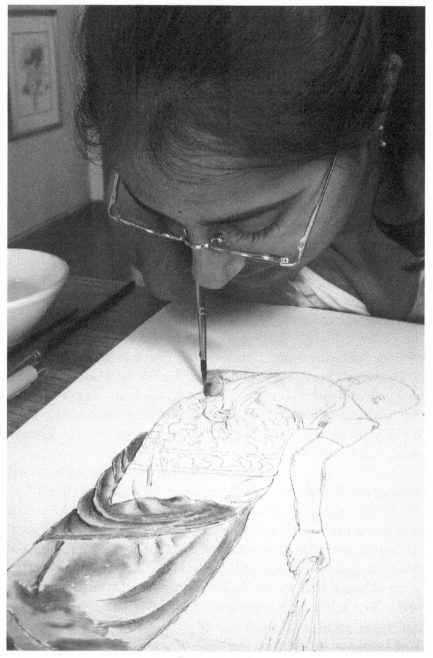

Painting, 2009

I dearly loved. That wasn't hard. In some ways, watercolor is an unforgiving medium. Nobody can just paint over a mistake and try to correct it without creating mud. I knew that, and so I was nervous about making mistakes. But oh, when watercolor is good, it is incredible! I loved the light and the transparency. I loved seeing one color flow across the paper, blending with others, so that wonderful new hues appeared in ways I hadn't even expected.

This is what I wrote at the time: "I think my greatest fear about my work is that somewhere along the way I will screw up on a particular thing in the painting and lose it all. When I do mess up, I get discouraged and don't know how to fix it. What needs to improve is my boldness with color. Quite a few of my paintings are very pale. They don't sparkle the way I want them to, because the colors aren't rich enough. Another of my roadblocks is that I am afraid that the message I want to give won't be understood or appreciated by the viewer. I always wonder what people are thinking when they see my work. Sometimes they look at a piece and seem deep in thought, or they ooh and aah loudly. But I want to know what they see in it, all the while hoping that the message I'm trying to give is the one they read into the picture."

I was barely beginning to understand that not even God can control how people "read" his creation. Not even God can control whether they understand the love and purpose that shine out of all He does. We all want so deeply to be heard, to be understood, to be known. Surely that is true of God, too.

That fall semester we added art history to the curriculum. Art Across Time by Laurie Adams became our textbook. She asked me to write several papers in which I was supposed to analyze artistic styles in different periods of history. I enjoyed the research and the actual writing far more than I had anticipated which surprised me. I realized that writing was another kind of art, an idea that hadn't ever occurred to me, although I had always liked to put my thoughts on paper. Emily wrote, "Her 8-10 page papers were a delight to grade. She has a beautiful way of writing and I think she will go far in writing…and someday would make an excellent art teacher."

The art of writing is still physically difficult for me. In those days it took a lot of time. Many people love voice-activated software, and a program is actually installed on my computer. However, I still prefer to scribble my thoughts by "hand" on notebook paper, using a pencil held between my shoulder and chin. Later on I type what I've written, tapping the keys with the end of a pencil, letter by letter. It's faster than you think! Sometimes I ask my mom to transcribe what I've written first, and then I can easily edit or change whatever I've composed. So for now, I have abandoned the voice software, just as I abandoned those arms and legs so long ago. It is probably for some of the same reasons, too. I like to feel what I am doing. Mom says artists just like their hands to get dirty. She may be right!

It takes courage to paint or draw, to create music or sculpture, to write a poem, play, or book. I suppose it even takes a certain amount of courage to make a fancy meal for guests, to wrap a present beautifully, to nurture children, or to plant a flower garden. Human creativity is common to us all – it's as normal as breathing, just as ordinary as a child's first scribble, and yet, thrilling. Our efforts to be creative reflect God's endless creativity, as does love. And both are risky.

To create freely, all of us have to discover ways to get ourselves out of the way. That means turning our focus away from ourselves so we aren't constantly worrying about how our work appears to others. Emily used to say, "Make God your only audience." I think what she meant was that if I did anything honestly, with my eye on integrity so that God would approve it as "the truth," then the audience response, whatever it was, would take care of itself.

The more I learned, the more urgently Emily worked with me to understand what art is really about. We read Scripture together. We prayed. She prayed for me. We worked through Walking on Water by Madeline l'Engle and Scribbling in the Sand by Michael Card. I began to take more time alone with God, deliberately and regularly, not just when I thought I had time.

Before I ever put pencil to paper, she taught me to ask, "What am I trying to communicate with this piece?" That question became a life question for me – What am I trying to express with my life? What do I want to say with this essay? What might God want to communicate

69

through my drawing? It was, and is, a constant challenge.

In the spring of 2005, just after I turned 17, Emily wrote, "Minda has really grown in her drawing techniques and has achieved what she never thought she could, or would even want to, in her drawings of people. She has a natural talent in drawing, I believe. Her drawings are exciting, energetic and strong. They show no fear!"

It is so important to have wise teachers and friends who see us before we see ourselves, who see more than we do, who can identify what God is doing in us before we know it ourselves, and who will speak those perceptions back to us.

If every young Christian had the kind of mentors I have had, what might our world be like? If each of us chose to be that kind of mentor to another, what might our world become?

CHAPTER THIRTEEN

GED

I stood there stunned. Emily's words rang loud and clear in my ears, "If you refuse to take the GED, then I will no longer give you art lessons." Emily had been telling me that I ought to go ahead and take the GED for a long time, but I didn't want to do it. I kept pushing the subject away. I just didn't see the point. There was no particular need for me to do it, I thought. I figured I could earn my living with my art, as I wanted to do. Being an artist was my dream, my pleasure, my great joy. I just didn't see anything else that really interested me. I was quite content with becoming the best artist I could be. Even my mom was okay with that. God can be glorified by anything, I knew. College is not necessary in order for someone to praise the Lord with honorable work. And if I wasn't going to go to college, which I emphatically was not, then why did I need to take the GED?

Emily persisted. "You're perfectly smart enough to do it, Minda." Well, maybe so, but why should I? It would mean taking GED classes, including math, which I had always found excruciatingly frustrating. Math ideas were hard, for one thing. I couldn't count on my fingers, so I had learned everything by sight, by visualizing addition and subtraction, fractions and division. The fact is numbers didn't show up in my visual imagination very well! Writing math problems always tormented me as well. Copying problems from the board or out of a book was really hard because I had to keep lifting my head from the paper, remembering what I saw, and then bending down low again to write. It was so easy to make a mistake, and so difficult to erase it all and go back to correct the error if I did. I hated math. I was not at all in the mood to pick up algebra and geometry again. I thought it was unfair for her to ask me to do it, and I said so. Repeatedly.

But Emily was not content. She kept pushing me week after week the entire fall semester until she finally uttered her terrible threat to stop teaching me altogether. That was more than I could bear. I looked forward to my Wednesday art lessons more than anything else in the world. It wasn't only learning to draw, use watercolors, and pay attention to detail that I loved. It was always more than that. I doubt that she really knew it, but my hours with Emily encouraged me to reframe my whole world. As she taught me how to look at every object in a painting in relation to every other object, I was also learning about the composition that is my life.

As I saw how every line and every color in a good painting or drawing had a reason to be there, God showed me a little of what He had been up to as He shaped my life as well. I was discovering how God was at work in me, creating my life as His careful and beautiful composition, with necessary dark shadows as well as areas of bright color. I recognized interesting textures, careful perspective, infinite variety and gentle repetition, all the things Emily had taught me to include in my own work. I was learning to trust God more confidently to complete what He had begun in me, and to call it "good." I needed her.

So I gathered up my courage, made the call, and had my mom drive me to the GED center on the SBU campus. Mom wouldn't have pushed me to do it. She wasn't even sure Emily should. Nevertheless, she was delighted when I made the decision to go ahead. I went into the classroom reluctantly, expecting the whole thing to be torture. But when I actually made up my mind to meet this goal, one that wasn't really even mine, I found that I wasn't afraid anymore.

When I chose to obey Emily's direction, I found it easier than I expected. Strangely, I actually enjoyed studying the hard things. Even math seemed almost possible, and the subjects I already liked, such as history, science, reading and writing, were just fun.

It was good to wheel into the GED center every day. Suddenly I was eager to take the exam and prove to myself that I could pass it. A great instructor helped. Joan Geltmacher has encouraged many others who have left school to take the GED and use it to fulfill their dreams. She surely encouraged me. It never occurred to her that I couldn't pass it.

Week by week I studied and practiced math on the computer as well as on paper. My confidence grew, as did my understanding of those strange numbers and how they worked. Math is not a language I like, but at least I began to make a little better sense of it, and to gain better control over it.

During April, just after my birthday in what would have been my senior year, mom drove me to Springfield to take the GED exam. It was kind of odd to be in a huge classroom all by myself. Because I write slowly, and sometimes have to stop for a while to give my back a break, I had been granted extra time to complete each section, which required that I be in a room all by myself. It took the pressure off, but as the first day wore on, I discovered that I didn't actually need that additional time after all. By the time I had finished the whole exam, I was ecstatic. I felt I had done well. I knew I had done my best. A few weeks later, about the time I would have graduated had I been in public school, I opened the large envelope and saw my certificate. I had passed all sections of the GED on my first try! I could hardly wait to call Emily with the good news. I had shown her I could do it. I was proud, I had saved my art classes, and I was finished – proud, happy, and done with school.

A few weeks later, I found myself in an unexpected, deep conversation with Emily's husband. Jim is about the gentlest man I know, and before I realized it, he was talking to me about taking a class at SBU – just one, of course, to see if I liked it. I listened, but I also resisted his suggestion. Although this time I knew better than to argue out loud!

"When Minda completed her GED, she was on a high because she had done what she never thought she could do as far as education is concerned. So Emily and I discussed what might be a next step for her growth and achievement. Since I was on faculty at SBU, and at heart we are both so passionate about students' growth and development, we naturally thought of Minda taking a college course. She was very hesitant about this next "impossibility." So I wondered what course could be really helpful to her spiritually, but not overwhelm her academically? "Spiritual Formation" taught by Tige Bennett would be a really great only-one-course-at-a-time college beginning. And because Minda was very tuned in to spiritual things, I was sure this course would hold her attention" (Dr. Jim Frost, March, 2013).

And so began a whole new chapter of my life – the best one yet.

Hopefully, you see what happens when someone discovers the joy of obedience, even reluctantly. One act of obedience leads to another invitation to obey, and that leads to yet another. I do not always do everything someone tells me to do. That would be foolish and dangerous. But Emily loved me and I trusted her. We tried to listen to God together, teacher and student. So I obeyed her.

Because she was paying more attention than I was, or simply had a different perspective than I did, she also had a better sense of what God might be doing in me and offering to me. I am pretty sure she guessed where that first obedience might take me – right into a fresh encounter with God that would lead me beyond the GED to SBU – and then to the world in Jesus' name.

That GED certificate became a symbol of faith. It represents something more powerful than it intends in itself. It's a picture of trust. It's a personal illustration of that old hymn, "Trust and obey, for there's no other way to be happy in Jesus, than to trust and obey." Freedom to obey God is God's gift of genuine, authentic liberation.

CHAPTER FOURTEEN

Graduation: The Art Show

During May of 2006, an article in the Bolivar newspaper announced the opening reception for Emergence, the title Emily and I had chosen for my first art show. As this event served to celebrate my home school graduation, we intended the title to suggest that I was emerging, along with my art, into a future where what I might become had not yet been revealed.

Somehow, Emily had arranged for us to use the beautiful space in the Driskill Art Gallery at SBU. The day before the show her husband cheerfully vacuumed the room, which took me completely by surprise. I'd never seen a man serve his wife like that, and it made a huge impression on me. As I watched, Emily and my mom laid out all my framed pieces on the floor along the walls, arranging and rearranging them over and over. She kept asking my opinion, trying to get my input, but I was too overwhelmed to say much of anything.

I drove my red wheelchair back and forth, staring at all those pieces, representing hundreds of hours of work, now visible to anyone who walked by. One of my favorites, A Balanced Life, depicted a strong Haitian woman striding along the path, carrying a basket of fruit on her head. I had done it because I wanted to honor Becca, my Haitian sister who lives her life with such courage and beauty. As I gazed at the woman's bright red dress, and thought about her obvious sturdy determination, I realized that I had communicated that very thing. It was real. What was on paper did tell a story. Anybody could see it and "read" it. My heart sang, but there were no words.

Emily told my mom what to do, and I vaguely noticed the two of them measuring spaces between paintings, making sure they were exactly right. I heard the sound of their hammering, talking and laughing. But I was too full to take it all in.

I stopped by my pencil drawing, Freedom, Ltd., an abstract self-portrait, which depicts both the "bars" and "chains" representing the limitation that my wheelchair imposes, but also the "wings" that that enable me to fly free because I have that chair. "Great is Thy Faithfulness," I sang over and over in my heart.

Nearby hung my other self-portrait done in charcoal – it was the image of a little girl painting one of those cheap plastic ornaments intended to be hung in a window, so the light can shine through the color. The drawing reproduced my first Christmas in Albuquerque, before I turned three. I was bent over the kitchen table, my hair in a tangled mess, carefully using my paint-filled brush to fill in a picture of Mary with the baby Jesus. The original ornament still hangs in my mother's kitchen window every Christmas, with sunshine still pouring through the fading red and blue. So many memories flooded my mind as I stared at that drawing, and gratitude bubbled up in me. What I had loved as a tiny child had been restored to me, pressed down, filled up and overflowing! All around me was proof of my love for art, and evidence that God had blessed me to do it. Every drawing and every painting told a story, and reminded me of a personal struggle I'd overcome, a difficult technique finally learned, or a happy accident of water and color.

Delicate red and gold tulips in an old can hung there, along with another watercolor of a winter-bare tree and a fiery purple and rose sunset spread across the sky. There was also the solemn pencil drawing of a young Navajo shepherdess. Everywhere I looked, my inner life shined out of the pieces neatly hanging against the walls, visible through the massive glass windows. Emily had talked about an artist's vulnerability; I finally knew what she meant.

There were silly, lighthearted moments that day as well. Emily showed me the purple ribbons, clearly representing SBU, which she had attached to my guest book. In spite of myself, I grinned. There was nothing subtle about that!

By the next evening, everything was ready. The women from St. Alban's Episcopal Church, my home congregation, provided a beautiful reception with tables piled with many kinds of home-baked desserts. One of the women had even made me a new, sophisticated black dress so I wouldn't feel quite so young and self-conscious. Friends had come from long distances to share this night, including Paul and Cyndy Teas from Camp Barnabas, and even mom's favorite Nazarene Seminary professor, Dr. Alex Deasley and his wife, Joyce.

But would anyone come who didn't know me already? And if they did, what would I say to them? Most of my artwork was for sale. Would anyone buy it? What if they did? Could I let all this hard work just disappear forever once my art show came down at the end of June? Would I ever be able to paint anything this good again? My mind raced with nervous excitement.

Slowly at first, and then in a rush, the lobby area filled with people. Everywhere I turned, someone wanted to congratulate me, ask a question, or make a comment on some piece that interested them. Noise swirled around me as everyone's kindness caught me and wrapped me in sheer joy. Before long, little round stickers began to appear all over the gallery, indicating that someone had bought a drawing or painting. I even overheard Emily talking to the social worker who had arranged my adoption so many years before, Barbara Knowles from Washington. My two friends had never met, but there they were, happily discussing which painting Barbara wanted to purchase.

All year I had been reflecting on Madeline L'Engle's writings, slowly learning to be a servant of the work that is drawing and painting. L'Engle taught me to see myself as a servant of God, and also a servant to God's people in my art. In my journal that year I'd written, "Being a servant is what God is asking me to become for others. It is what I want my artwork to do for other people, too, to serve them by offering a place to rest, a peaceful space." It was never as easy as it sounds to take my eyes off myself, to stop being focused on every little mistake or imperfection, and to offer myself and my work to my Master so that He could bless others through it. That night I was glad for the struggle, really glad. And it seemed others were glad, too.

Right in front of me stood dozens of generous people, each an illustration of what a servant's heart looks like. They chose to come, chose to buy paintings, but mostly they came to thank me and Emily for doing this work together, teacher and student. They came happily and eagerly: Kathy Brown and her husband, Dana Hacker, friends from church, Rivendell Community members, even my GED teacher. All the people whose lives had impacted mine came freely to serve me with their praise and delight in what I had accomplished. No one deserves that. I knew it. But I drank it all in, too. It wasn't their praise that I hungered for, it was the affirmation that I had heard rightly, that all this work wasn't a waste of time. That God really was in the midst of my art. I thought of Chariots of Fire, one of my favorite movies. "When I run, I feel God's pleasure," Eric Liddell says, when someone challenges how his love of running fits into his Christian future. Liddell became a missionary to China and used his love of sport to encourage and teach young men about the love of God. "This is my 'way,'" I breathed. And God is pleased."

The training had been rigorous, and it was not over. It's not just the technical aspects of learning to use different media, how to handle charcoal without making a mess, or how to keep watercolors transparent and vivid at the same time. It wasn't just figuring out how to mat and frame my pieces, although that aspect of presentation is an art all by itself. It wasn't even choosing subject matter and working through problems of composition and perspective, accuracy and originality. It was all deeper than that. To be an artist, or an Olympic champion like Eric Liddell, or even a tough, supportive mom like mine, is to be ready every single day to begin again. That's not genius, it is ordinary hard work. I tried to say some of that to the reporters who asked why I did what I do.

But it's what I said about Emily that brings me to tears, because it is so true. "Emily has given me feet to walk with. She's given me light to see that I, too, can be a light in the world…I look at her and I can see the face of God. I can see the love of God in her. I can see what God is like – an encourager and a shepherd and the helper of the one trying to create" (The Lebanon Daily Record, June 18, 2006).

Here's what I know for sure:

A teacher who doesn't love her student is mostly worthless in shaping character, even if the student gains facts and techniques and competence in a field.

A teacher who loves a student is a wonderful gift to any learner, and sets the student free to follow in her footsteps.

But any teacher who loves God first, and passionately, who then loves the student with the passion of God's love, is the one who sets the student free to follow the Lord God wherever He leads.

CHAPTER FIFTEEN

Emerging

Jim had encouraged me to register for a single class. Emily insisted on it. Mom told me to do whatever I thought God wanted me to do, but she assured me that we could manage if I decided to try. All summer I hesitated, but finally we drove to town and I signed up for one class. I took Jim's advice and chose Spiritual Formation. So when August rolled around, although I was still studying art with Emily, I also spent a couple of hours each week at SBU. I'd sold most of my paintings and drawings at my senior art exhibit, so I could pay the tuition. Oh, there were a few people who told me that if I really wanted to go to college, I ought to go to a state school where everything was cheaper, but it wasn't "school" I wanted. It was to be part of a particular community that had already reached out and welcomed me. I wanted to "belong" to SBU.

It surprises me now to remember just how anxious and shy I was that first day of class. Dr. Bennett put me at ease immediately. She cheerfully dragged a table over in front of the board, so I'd have a place to park my wheelchair, see what was happening, and be able to take notes. In about three minutes I'd made up my mind – she was going to be terrific. Her class definitely held my attention! Tige was full of energy and enthusiasm; when she asked a question, she wasn't interested in pat, cheap, or "Sunday School" answers. She wanted to know what we really thought about God and His involvement in our own lives. Her assignments challenged me, and delighted me, too. I had naturally worried a little about how a committed Episcopalian, whose mom is the local Episcopal priest, would fit into a Southern Baptist school. The short answer turned out to be, "Easily!" Tige probed my faith, but she did the same with Baptists. Her goal was to push us all more deeply into the love of God, and into a fuller response to the gospel of Jesus, the Lord. I was definitely up for that, and I loved every single class.

"Well, she completed that course so well, really well, that I recommended that the next, only-one-course-at-a-time class be New Testament History in the spring semester, which she could take from me. She knew me already, and that gave her some needed confidence. This course was more academic, but if she needed help, I could give her that help. And again, she completed all the readings and the exams and passed the course wonderfully with a great deal of study on her part. She was thrilled" (Jim Frost, March, 2013).

I was thrilled, but not just at the end of the course when I saw that coveted, "A." I was thrilled from the first day. Aside from studying something about the cultures and geography of the time, as well as the history of biblical interpretation and translation, we read the entire New Testament, cover to cover. I had never sat down and read it straight through before, and it soon became pretty obvious that hardly anyone else in the class had, either. Book by book we read, discussed, argued amongst ourselves, and listened to Dr. Frost lecture on every single part of it. The Baptists were surprised by some of what they found in the text, and so was I. All of us had heard the gospel of course, but it was seeing the whole picture unfold right before us, watching the captivating and sometimes perplexing portrait of Jesus, and then of the emerging Church, that thrilled me. Dr. Frost required us to write short, personal reflections in response to every single day's Bible readings. Those exercises helped me organize my quiet thoughts into printed paragraphs, and made them clearer in my own mind. Dr. Frost read them all, too, because he would often scribble an observation or a question about something I wrote. I've kept most of those papers for years, because those assignments taught me how to look for the unexpected, to read carefully whatever was in front of my eyes. That lesson was invaluable.

I had been learning the same thing in art – to see. Before I began to draw I hadn't noticed how much of what is all around me lay outside my awareness. Now I saw that I had spent a lot of time just reading passages I'd never even stopped to examine. My mom used to always say, "Minda, pay attention," when she realized I was dreaming my own dreams instead of focusing on whatever she was saying. Suddenly, I understood. Scripture became alive, challenging, confirming, correcting my hazy perceptions about God's intentions for the world, and for me.

I began speaking up in class when I had something to contribute. I discovered to my surprise that the college students that seemed so confident and so vastly superior to me when I walked in the door were actually just as ordinary as I was. They accepted me as ordinary, too. I began making friends who didn't pay much attention to the wheelchair, or to the fact that I had no legs or arms, but who focused a lot more on diet coke, fries and cramming for Dr. Frost's impossible exams. For me, that was sheer joy.

My art didn't suffer either, as I had feared. In fact, I painted even better and worked just as hard. My whole world just kept opening up. Every time I walked a little farther in the path of trust and love, the more there was to see.

That first taste of college had been wonderful. My single toe was in SBU water for sure and rapidly turning purple. SBU t-shirts were easier for me to wear than most anything else, a lot more comfortable than dresses, and just as long. I bought a dozen different ones of all colors. Once the sleeves had been cut out and the side seams corrected, I became a rolling advertisement for SBU wherever I went. And I was proud to belong, even just a little, to that great school.

As soon as the fall semester began again in 2007, Jim and Emily invited me to attend the Intercultural Studies (ICS) retreat, since the ICS majors were all gathering at Rivendell for the weekend. I met one of my best SBU friends there, Sarah Simmonds. I enjoyed the fellowship, the games and singing, the drama, and the prayer. We played out the story of Jesus raising Lazarus from death. We used many outdoor acres to carve out space for curious villagers to gather around grieving Mary, and for impetuous Martha to run to meet Jesus, who really did have to walk with his friends on a dusty road to get to our imagined tomb in "Bethany." I saw it all newly – that Mary had no idea what Jesus and Martha were saying to each other, and that Jesus' disciples didn't know what was going on back at the house. I loved being part of that activity, because it helped me understand how drama works as a language for speaking the truth that is Jesus. We listened to reports from students who had returned from their six-months abroad, visited with a representative of the International Mission Board, and prayed for the nations. That ICS weekend opened my heart to the possibility of serving Christ somehow cross-culturally. In a way, that awareness was almost a natural outgrowth of my previous interests and experiences in an international family. It seemed as if God had been preparing me for years to hear that invitation.

Emily used to give me quotes to hang on the wall in my studio, things that would force me to stop and think. She knew I was at risk of "playing to my audience" because my senior art show had been so successful. It was easy to want to paint what I had painted before, things that I knew people liked. It was hard to go beyond it and try something different. So one of the first quotes she gave me before I started my first SBU class read, "Don't ask yourself what the world needs, but ask yourself what makes you come alive, and then do that. What the world needs is people who are alive" (anonymous).

Tige had asked me that, too, in so many ways. "What's the bottom line?" she would ask. Or, "How is that working for you?" No matter what any of us said in class, it was clear that Dr. Frost cared about more than filling our brains with details (although he did that too, infuriatingly!). He wanted to know our hearts, whether we were engaging the New Testament, growing in faith, and trusting God enough to put our whole weight on the Truth who is also Life. So what "makes me come alive?" The love of God in Christ Jesus, our Lord. How would I "do" or "show" God's love? I was still figuring that out.

During November, Emily and I had another art exhibit, but this time it featured work we had both done that year. It was a proud moment when I looked up and saw my pieces hanging next to hers.

Even though I didn't take any classes that semester, I participated in the ICS Bible study at the Frost's house on Sunday evenings, and made a few more friends. I knew I wasn't exactly like them. They lived in the dorms, were involved in all kinds of social activities, and were all self-assured. I was shy, awkward, and usually perfectly happy to just sit and watch what was going on, or to talk with someone I already knew. Still, those were precious times, ordinary times. My heart continued to open, my future to emerge.

Oddly, for someone who had once been so afraid of the University, I missed being on campus. But there was a good reason why I wasn't. Instead of taking another class that fall, Jim, Emily, my mom and I were planning a trip to India, so I was busy painting, drawing, and printing hundreds of Christmas cards to pay for it.

CHAPTER SIXTEEN

Christmas

In early spring my mom had gotten the word – Ashraya was planning a huge celebration for their 25th anniversary in late December, 2007. Adoptees and their families from Sweden, Italy and the U.S. had all been invited to return to Bangalore for the festivities. Ashraya, which means shelter, had been my home for fifteen months before mom brought me to the U.S., and I was desperate to go and see it for myself. So I saved all my money, sold as many of my watercolors and drawings as I could, and made Christmas cards to pay for the trip. There was no way I was going to miss this!

Still, you can probably imagine that traveling such a distance with me is no easy thing. Handling my manual wheelchair, keeping track of baggage, finding taxis and locating the least inaccessible path forward is not a one-person job. Somehow I convinced Jim and Emily to come along. We needed help, but we also wanted their company. We had laughed, planned, purchased tickets, sent emails back and forth to India, and gotten our shots. Everything was in place.

Christmas Eve was beautiful that year. A real infant slept on the straw in our life-size manger at church. Flaming poinsettias and lighted candles shone in the quiet darkness. We sang carols and heard the great Story, hugged each other and shared Communion. Many of our friends gathered around me after the service to encourage us and promise their prayers. We opened gifts. Mom had made me a new blouse for my silk sari, and Emily had even given me an Indian silver and jade necklace that had once belonged to her mother.

But by Christmas afternoon, I was having a hard time. My stomach was all butterflies, and even though the tree was still bright and Christmas music filled the house, I was barely aware of any of it. My heart was already far away. Mom had to keep pulling me out of my daydreams so I could pack my allergy meds, gather up the gifts for the orphanage staff, and find the extra camera batteries. I could hardly eat for excitement. And sleep? Forget it. As for prayer, all I could manage was, "Thank you!" Just repeating the word India made my heart sing. I could hardly wait!

Only a few days later the plane set us down in Delhi on the first leg of our journey south to Bangalore. Quickly, everything became more complicated than I had expected. Maybe you can picture what it took to get me in and out of small Indian planes. More than once I found myself perched outside in my wheelchair on the airline's moveable stairs, unable to hang on to anything, being passed down dozens of steep steps to the ground. But Jim was always there with a hand on my shoulder to reassure me as he directed the men. We teased him, calling him the "bag boy" because he handled all of our luggage. But mostly, and more importantly, Jim kept me safe.

I couldn't believe it when we shared our first meal in Bangalore with all the others who had come to celebrate! It was amazing. I love my University a lot. But really, it's a little hard to blend in with a bunch a of SBU blondes. Here, everywhere I looked, I saw myself. Things were familiar in other ways, too. I seemed to remember certain foods, particular smells, even the soft sounds of Hindi and Kannada. It really made me smile to see other people moving their heads exactly as I sometimes do, to indicate that they were listening. The loud music blaring from buses and boom boxes sounded like music I'd heard before.

It must be true that a baby's first two years shape her "self" deeply, in ways no one can fully understand. I was twenty-two months old when I left Bangalore, and now, nearly eighteen years later it seemed exactly like what I imagined "home" to be. Of course, not every child whose parents cannot care for her finds the kind of shelter that Ashraya was for me. Most do not. Too many lost or abandoned children still wander the streets of our world, or struggle to survive in orphanages where children are little loved. Too many simply die. But the same gentle women who had bathed and fed and played with me as a baby were still caring for babies at Ashraya. The social workers who founded it still worked to assure security and hope for the orphaned and abandoned, but also for children of construction workers, for abused women, for rural families. I was proud to be an "Ashraya baby." I still am. That shelter was an experience of God's protection. In that home I experienced grace long before I knew the word. Already God was surrounding me with His love through Hindu, Parsi and other Christian women, preparing me to trust Him, and equipping me for an intercultural future no one could have imagined then.

I loved hearing the ayahs tell stories about my shy smiles and curious nature, and about learning my first English word, "Hello!" They told me how I had screamed at the sight of my new mother, until she fed me my favorite jelly candy. It was great fun to find that a couple of the older adoptees who were with us at the reunion remembered playing with me as a toddler, teaching me to roll from one place to another since obviously I couldn't crawl. All of that helps explain why I had adapted so easily to my new family. Children who are loved well in those early years are usually able to thrive in a new environment, to attach to their new families, and to find a new place of belonging. Certainly that was true for me.

Emily and I had been invited to lead an art workshop for everyone on the second day of the gathering. Before we left Bolivar, we decided to have everyone make a large quilt of heavy watercolor paper. Everyone painted whatever they liked, and several people stitched all the pieces together, finally hanging the huge quilt just in time for the New Year's Eve party. I'd never tried to lead a group activity before, but I was surprised at how confident I felt speaking. It was so cool to see the staff from Ashraya painting alongside the children and young adults as they were telling stories, talking and laughing. Emily walked around encouraging everybody, while mom mostly took pictures. It was good she did because for me, the whole trip became one spectacular kaleidoscope of bright color, fascinating people, and surprising opportunities, continually shifting and changing in the light.

On the itinerary that Jim made for our trip, he listed the possibility of traveling to Manipal/Udupi to visit my birth family after our time in Bangalore. More than anything, I wanted to do that. But on New Year's Eve, the director of Ashraya, Nomita Chandy, wisely and firmly discouraged me. Not all reunions with birthparents work out very well in the first place, and she was pretty sure this one was going to be impossible anyway.

During the New Year's Eve party, I "danced" to loud music with all the others, ate plenty of delicious holiday food, and hung out with my new friends. But inside, I was miserable. Emily came to our room late that night and strongly urged me to stop acting helpless. She was still confident that somehow, in some way, God would show us how to work it out if I was really determined to find my family. She told me to make up my mind whether I was really going to push forward to locate my parents and then do all I could to make that meeting happen, or to stop and let that dream go. It was my choice, she said. I didn't know what to do. It scared me to stand up to someone with power and simply insist to Mrs. Chandy that I wanted desperately to find my parents, and that I needed her help. I finally I made up my mind. If there was anything I could do, I was going to do it.

Two days later, each adoptee met with the Ashraya staff, who gave us copies of all the information they had in their records, although that wasn't enough. Mrs. Chandy told me again that there was only a 2% chance of finding my family unless we could get more information from the hospital that had relinquished me to Ashraya so long ago. I picked up my courage and told her exactly why this mattered so much – I knew there was no way I could come back to India easily, or soon, even if someone located my parents later. This was my only time to do it. There had to be a way. I stood my ground, and then I held my breath. The sky didn't fall. No one got angry. Mrs. Chandy just stared at me.

The next morning, our last scheduled day in Bangalore, we decided to drop by Ashraya once again. I wanted to say goodbye and to leave the painting I had made for my mother along with the letter I had written her. Perhaps someday Ashraya would finally get the information they needed to find my mother after all. But when we arrived, we found photographers and reporters from the local newspapers waiting to talk to me. Mrs. Chandy had called them the afternoon before, after we talked, hoping that publicizing my desire might help. She thought that someone who read the paper might know something about my family, since rural people often migrate to cities like Bangalore for work.

All day long I answered questions. I let myself be photographed over and over, sometimes with the Ashraya children, sometimes with Emily or my mom, and once with the painting I'd made for my mother. It was hard to satisfy so many photographers and reporters all at once, but it was also necessary. I remembered what Emily had told me.

When we finally drove away to stay with some Indian friends overnight, Mrs. Chandy urged us to remain in Bangalore another day just to see what would happen. The next morning mom got a frantic message to call Ashraya. "Things have been happening," Mrs. Chandy finally told her, "like, for instance, her family has been located!"

When I finally got back to Ashraya, my sister Pavithra stood waiting, a shy seventeen-year-old who worked at a garment factory in Bangalore that was owned by my uncle. I could hardly believe it. Pavithra held me and cried, upset that her mother had not kept me at home. It was hard to explain that everything was okay, that I wasn't angry, but that I was just excited to see her and to find our parents. My mother's younger brother was there, too. His English was better than Pavithra's, so he helped us talk to each other. As we did, one of the social workers realized that my family lived in a village just a few kilometers from her village. She spoke their language, of course, and her uncle was the postmaster for the whole area, including my parents' village. A cell phone call sent him out of his office and out to the tiny village of Kolekebailu to find them and tell them that I was in India and eager to meet them. They must have been stunned. I certainly was! Twenty-four hours later, hearing that indeed my family wanted to see me, Jim got busy and made plane reservations for the very next day. Emily and mom cheered. I can't even express how I felt.

I was glad, but also humbled. God had known all along what He was going to do for me. God didn't need my help, of course, He had

89

done it all. But somehow, it was necessary for me to ask for what I wanted, and to "do all I could." That's a couple of lessons, I guess. Emily had wanted me to learn them both – to step out with determination and do everything possible, and then to trust God no matter what. It wasn't the last time I would need to put those lessons into practice. Of all the things she has ever taught me about art or about God, these might be the most important.

The morning we were to fly across the state, I suddenly realized I needed to buy gifts. We tried to figure out what to get and where to shop, but before we could do it another large constituent of my extended family arrived with flowers and gifts of jewelry, as well as questions galore for me, my mom, and the staff of Ashraya. I never did figure out exactly who they all were, but it was pretty amazing to be surrounded by "my" people, especially the older women who gazed at me carefully to be sure I was really their own. We were running out of time by then, so Emily and Jim quietly left in the midst of all the visiting and went to do the shopping for me. They returned with gorgeous purple silk for my mother's new sari, material for a shirt for my dad, and things for my two younger sisters. The gifts were exactly right.

The Christmas decorations in Bangalore were still up everywhere on this fifth of January. It was "Twelfth night" at home, the day we usually celebrate the last day of the Christmas season with a party. But this year, the best gifts were still to come!

CHAPTER SEVENTEEN

Epiphany

I woke up early the next morning in a hotel in Manipal, still surrounded by gold and red Christmas decorations. Lying very still under the stiff white sheets, I pretended to be sound asleep. Today, today, today beat my heart. Excitement about meeting my parents was all mixed up with my natural shyness and anxiety. What if they don't like me? What if they think I'm ugly?

Soon, my mom urged me out of bed so she could gather my hair into a single thick braid down my back. Nervously I tried to decide what to wear, finally settling on a beautiful, blue salwar kameez threaded with gold, and a matching dupatta. The gold was deliberate. On January 6, Epiphany, an even older feast than Christmas, begins to celebrate the coming of the Persian magi, the wise men who brought the child Jesus gifts in recognition of his yet-undeclared Kingship. Only those foreigners saw what God had revealed in Christ Jesus. It seemed right to celebrate that day by wearing just a bit of His royal gold. I wondered, too, what God would reveal to me this day, what I would see more clearly about Him, and what new things I might see about myself.

As we crawled into the van, I felt sort of like a Christmas package, sent by special delivery to a family anxiously waiting its arrival. When my parents relinquished me for adoption, they had no idea that I'd be gently wrapped up in my new family's love, one day prepared by God to return to thank them for their gift of my life. It was important to me to be the kind of present they would be proud to open, glad to receive. The truth was I didn't know if I was the gift they longed for, and I was scared.

At first, the van bumped along on ordinary paved roads. Jim and Emily tried to calm me down, the reporter and photographer kept talking to encourage me, and the driver kept up a cheerful patter. My mom sat beside me and kept her arm around my shoulder. Not much helped. We had driven for nearly an hour when Reshma's cell phone rang for the third time. She laughed into the receiver, speaking rapid Kannada. "It's your father again," she finally said, "He keeps calling to ask, 'When will I see my daughter?'" My father, I repeated to myself, my dad. Suddenly I could hardly wait to get to the village!

Not quite twenty years before, on April 11, 1988, I had been born in that village to Shankar and Kalavathi Shetty. I was their first, eagerly anticipated child. The whole village celebrates a woman's first pregnancy, and everyone waits to see the newborn. I can't begin to imagine what my mother's grief must have been, or what shock she must have felt when I emerged armless and legless. Did she feel shame, too? I don't know. But this I do know – my father himself carried me to the hospital in Manipal, many miles and a long bus ride away, seeking help for me. It was, and is, remarkable.

Just that week in Bangalore we read newspaper articles about abandoned baby girls, or dead ones found drowned or smothered. If even a healthy girl is sometimes a financial burden poor families simply cannot afford, what might my parents have felt about me? And yet, easy as it would have been to let me die, they didn't allow that to happen. Instead, my dad took me to the hospital, left his real name, my mother's, and the name of the village where they lived. It was an astonishing act of grace. They loved me. They claimed me. And my adoptive mother never let me forget it.

Months later, when they realized that no medical intervention would give me arms or legs, they reluctantly left me in Manipal, unable to care for me in the village. "Someday you will meet them, Minda," mom had always promised, "and when you do, you will be proud of them. They loved you. Never doubt that." My very life was proof she was right.

We drove through Karnataka's rich green fields, marveling at the beauty. We even caught a glimpse of the shining ocean. But the van finally had to slow. The paved roads petered out to dirt, and soon we

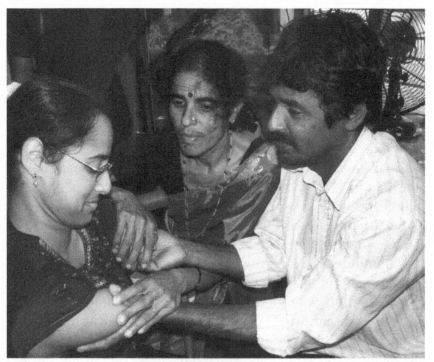

With my parents in India, 2008

noticed people walking, biking or running along beside the van. "They want to see you!" grinned Reshma. "Everyone has a cell phone, and they know Kalavathi's baby is coming!"

Finally, we entered a tiny path and stopped. Women wearing brightly colored saris, children dancing with excitement, and men, too, all surrounded the van, craning their necks and shoving each other to see me first. Once again, Jim became my rescuer and protector. "Get her mother," he insisted. "She wants her mother."

The crowd slowly parted to let her through. There was such fear in her eyes. She shyly reached out for my arm, but in an instant I pulled her right into my embrace. For a moment I felt as if I were comforting my own child. There we were, both of us clinging to each other and talking at once, neither understanding the other, Reshma doing her best to translate for us both. My grandmother stood just behind my mother, ready to protect her if needed, and Emily and my mom were behind me, in case things went badly. I think everyone was a little afraid one of us would be rejected by the other.

I was so grateful that Ashraya had let Reshma come with us. We needed her social work skills to reassure my parents, and we definitely needed her ability to translate. She told me that my mother had been crying ever since she heard I was coming, afraid that I would be angry with her, or ashamed of their poverty. As my mother tried to beg forgiveness for relinquishing me, I tried to thank her for saving my life. A couple of dogs were barking and snarling outside the van. It was hot and nobody could hear anything. It was totally chaotic. But I was tearfully, perfectly, happy.

Finally, Jim lifted me into my wheelchair, and my father pushed me into their little cement house. They had been busy, too, since they found out I was coming. Somehow my dad had gotten small gifts for me, and plates of fruit and flowers for Jim, Emily and my mom. My mother brought us food and was delighted to see me enjoy it. My beautiful, old grandmother sat calmly in a corner of the room, surveying everything as it unfolded. My little sisters eventually wandered off with Emily, who wanted to see everything. Jim and my father tried to keep the curious and very noisy crowd out of the house, but that was hopeless. If Jim closed one window, they just pushed open another; if my dad shut the front door, they just came in the back! Finally, my father had to wheel me out on the porch so that the curious crowd could come and touch me or smile to greet me. Some put flowers in my hair or on my lap.

Mostly, I sat by my mother and looked at her, as she looked at me. We tried to talk, but there was so much to say and most of it didn't need words, anyway. Her wedding picture hung on the wall behind her. She was exactly my age when she married my dad. The photo could have been of me. "It is good he took you when you were only one day old," my mother told me. "If he had waited until you were two days old I would not have let you go." And I knew it was true.

My father has worked hard since the early days of their marriage when all they had was a mud hut. He owns a small store at the edge of the village, and has built their cement house with its tiled roof.

He purchased their two cows and a few chickens, and kept all his daughters in school despite the prejudice against educating village girls. He is charming, cheerful, and I loved him at once. Chaitra and Pallavi were adorable. I'd never had younger sisters before, being the youngest in my adoptive family. It was a little strange to hear them call me akka, "older sister!"

In late afternoon we finally drove away. Jim made arrangements for my family to come the next day to the hotel in Manipal. We wanted to spend some quiet time with them away from the confusion and excitement of the crowds. Because I was sad to leave my mother's house, and because we all needed some way to relax after the excitement of the day, we went to the beach. I'd never seen the ocean, and it frightened me a little, but Jim took me straight into the water and let the waves break all over me. I could see far out into the sea, farther than I'd ever seen before, as the sun slowly sank leaving golden streaks in the waves. I loved the sound of the ocean, the taste of salt water – I loved it all. It was a perfect ending to a perfect day.

When my family arrived the next morning, I was astonished. My mother had already made her new blouse and was wearing the purple and silver sari I'd given her. Someone had made my dad's shirt, too. They were both so proud, and my mother looked like a queen. The girls were sweet, talkative and eager to try out their English. All of us tried to compress nineteen years into a few hours. There was tenderness, sorrow and joy all at once. Jim had arranged a private dining room so that we could eat undisturbed, free from the inevitable stares. We laughed a lot, but even that was poignant, because every minute brought us closer to the end. When the CNN-IBN reporter unexpectedly arrived to speak to my mother, she sat there smiling, no longer shy but poised and confident. "I have seen my child. Now I am content," she told them. Before they returned to the village, my mother bought a tiny silver bracelet and put it on my ankle. We embraced again and again. Then it was over – farewells and tears in the middle of a busy street.

What had been revealed to me? What was my epiphany in those

days? God is for us. God is with us, but God is also for us, on our side. He works all things for our good – for the good of us all. There is no situation outside His control and His love. And therefore, God can be trusted. Completely.

God is my true Father, and my dad is my father, too. I am my Indian mother's real daughter. I am also my American mom's real daughter. I know who I am. And all is well.

CHAPTER EIGHTEEN

Ramabai Mujti Mission

"A life totally committed to God has nothing to fear, nothing to lose, and nothing to regret." – Pandita Ramabai

Upon leaving Bangalore, we headed to Pune. We spent a few days with two SBU students, Intercultural Studies majors doing their six-months abroad, before traveling inland to Kedgaon to visit the Ramabai Mukti Mission. For several years, Emily's father served on the American Council of the Mission, and it was on a visit to Kedgaon that he purchased the jade necklace Emily gave me before we left Bolivar. So Jim and Emily were especially eager to see the place where her father had recognized the work of Christ in the Indian Church. My mom and I were also enthusiastic about this part of our journey.

My interest was in Ramabai herself, born in my own state of Karnataka in 1858. Although she was a woman, she was also a brilliant Brahmin scholar, earning the title Pandita (teacher) when she was barely twenty. She had surprised everyone with her rare mastery of the Hindu scriptures and the Sanskrit language. But soon after, Ramabai became frustrated by the attitude towards women from the Hindu scripture scholars. She traveled to England intending to study medicine to help alleviate the suffering of women and girls in India. While she was there, Ramabai read the Gospel for the first time. Soon she became a believer in Christ and was baptized. However, Ramabai stubbornly refused to join any western denomination.

When she returned to India, she kept her Hindu name, Ramabai, and the title she had been given, Pandita, refusing to become like a foreigner. She first opened a school for Brahmin child-widows because they could not re-marry or return to their parents. Instead, without education, they had to live as beggars. She also organized relief efforts during famine years, bringing more than 2,000 women and girls by train from across India to Kedgaon to keep them from starving. Ramabai began to translate the New Testament into Marathi, which she published in 1913. During that time, she continued to welcome abandoned girls, blind children and homeless women to her Mission, where they were nurtured and educated, and many made decisions for Jesus Christ. But everything was done by Indian standards, by Indian workers, and in Indian ways. She even had Indian musicians write entirely new hymns in Marathi for her girls using Indian instruments, melodies and rhythms.

Ramabai insisted on indigenization of the Gospel before almost anyone else even thought of it. She wrote, "Let the revival come to Indians so as to suit their nature and feelings. God has made them, He knows their nature, and He will work out His purpose in them in a way which may not conform to the ways of Western people and their lifelong training. Let the English and other missionaries begin to study the Indian nature – I mean the religious inclinations, the emotional side of the Indian mind" (Ramabai, Mukti Prayer Bell, Vol. II No.4, October, 1905).

That sounds a lot like what Jim taught us in our Intercultural Studies classes at SBU, about a hundred years later, but it was uncommon thinking in her day. In the late 1800s, nationalists criticized her because she had abandoned Hinduism, and Christian missionaries criticized her because she denied their authority to interpret "authentic" Christianity to Indians! In response, she wrote, "I am, it is true, a member of the Church of Christ, but I am not bound to accept every word that falls down from the lips of priests or bishops.... I have just with great efforts freed myself from the yoke of the Indian priestly tribe, so I am not at present willing to place myself under another similar yoke."

Ramabai appealed to me because I was trying to find my own way as an Episcopalian in a Baptist University, an Indian in an American home, and a disabled woman in an able-bodied world. I liked that she chose to be her ordinary self, and to follow Jesus in a way that fit her.

When we arrived, I was still full to the brim with my experience in Karnataka. I just kept thinking of those few days with my family, and of all I had seen and heard. I didn't expect anything more than to be with Emily as she visited the people she had known about for so many years, to enjoy seeing the Mission, and to enjoy the rest of the journey we had planned. I had no idea how deeply Mukti (which means "freedom") and the influence of Ramabai were going to affect me. Of course, I hardly ever know in advance what God is going to show me, or how He will use me, or how any situation is going to re-shape my life.

We hadn't been at Mukti for ten minutes before I saw Ramabai's motto on the wall – "A life totally committed to God has nothing to fear, nothing to lose and nothing to regret." About three minutes later, the director gave us a schedule for the next few days, including the expectation that I would speak repeatedly to various groups. Oh, help, I thought. Meeting my family had been such a tremendous joy, such a gift of God, and I wanted some time to process it all. And I was sad; it hadn't been easy to leave them. And now, unexpectedly, I was supposed to be cheerful and ready to tell others about Jesus. But right then, I just wasn't in the mood. I knew perfectly well that it was the love of God that gave me those days with my parents, and it was the same love that brought us to Mukti, but I still had trouble letting thoughts of my family take a back seat to these new people and their needs. I did not yet know that when I relinquished my own desire, and instead made room for the next thing God had for me, He would open up a whole new way of understanding my life.

One afternoon, tired from interacting with people all morning, I was lying down trying to take a nap when once again, someone knocked on the door and said that a group had gathered and was waiting for me. I was irritated. Right then God reminded me of a conversation I'd had with Emily about how crowds of people followed Jesus all the time, whether He was tired or hungry, in the mood to be friendly or not. We had read the stories in Matthew together and saw how no matter what was happening, Jesus "was filled with compassion" when He saw people's needs. Well, if He "was filled," it must mean that Jesus allowed God to fill Him. Emily's words were in my ears that afternoon. "Minda, it is important to remember that we are not our own Master, and that we are to be learning from Him. We are His servants." I had just a few minutes to turn toward Him and acknowledge that I was filled with my own concerns right then, and needed to be "filled with compassion." But it only takes a minute to turn when we are willing to do it, and it takes less time than that for God to answer and give us what we need most. On the outside, nothing had changed. The flowers in the courtyard were exactly the same beautiful pink blowing in the gentle air, the birds still sang, and Jim's smile was just the same as he wheeled me into the classroom where girls were waiting. But something had shifted in me. I spoke, and discovered that when I obeyed, I was in truth, "filled with compassion."

Sometimes Jim made it easier by standing next to me and asking questions, interviewing me instead of leaving me to come up with something fresh for each different group. Soon I saw that my words, awkward as they were, encouraged old women whose families had abandoned them, as well as blind women, disabled children, and even teenagers. I realized again that God could use me to tell, as well as to paint, His grace, His beauty, and His saving love.

As a teen, I had been about as self-conscious as anybody else, maybe more so because it was hard for me to blend in or to get lost in a crowd. Anonymity was always impossible for me, even though I craved it. Everywhere I went people looked at me twice; sometimes they just stared, often they made rude comments. Secure as a child, I became shy as I grew into adolescence. When I started drawing and painting, art became a kind of refuge, because I could make something beautiful without having to be visible myself. At least it had started that way.

But in India I began to see that God found my disability especially useful to Him. I gave my testimony over and over at Mukti and as I did, I slowly relaxed and saw myself connect with people who needed to know what God could do for them. God gave me a glimpse of myself using my voice as well as my art, my disabled body as well as my pen and ink to serve Jesus. I decided I wanted to tell the good news of Jesus in my own way, to people who lived without hope.

I discovered that as long as I thought I had something to lose by my obedience, or something to fear, my life was still far from the total commitment that characterized Ramabai. Her words haunted me, encouraged me, and became a kind of barometer for me.

CHAPTER NINETEEN

Intercultural Studies–Baby Steps

The trip to India focused my vision and gave me opportunities I had never imagined. I had not expected to be asked to speak to other internationally adopted young adults I'd never met, to tell them about my art, and to assure them that God has given us all gifts to use for others. But I did, and found it wasn't terrifying at all.

I didn't anticipate all the public interest in me, or in how I was living happily with a disability. The crush of reporters and their very personal questions surprised me. But as I began answering them, I found the freedom to do it. I'd never even been in a factory before, and yet I talked to young men and women who were leaders in an Indian company in Bangalore, demonstrating how I write and draw, and sharing examples of my artwork. I realized with shock that they seemed to appreciate what I had to say.

Once we arrived at Mukti Mission and realized that the Director had scheduled me to speak repeatedly during the next few days, I was overwhelmed. But by the end of the week, I knew for sure that whatever my future was going to be, drawing and painting wasn't the whole of it. The desire to speak out of my heart and to tell others that God is good to all of us all the time had been born in me and was growing.

We returned to Bolivar too late for me to take a class that semester, and my money was spent anyway. So I poured myself into my art, painting and drawing what I had seen and learned and loved in India. As I drew, I thought, reflected, and prayed about what my life meant, and what God created me to create by living that life.

It seemed wonderful to again dip my brush into wet, vivid color and paint a sari or a baby on his mother's back. I completed three of my favorite paintings that spring, watercolors of strong Indian women going about their ordinary work. As I worked, I tried to imagine what their real lives were like. That helped me remember that these women were real people with friends, families, and their own worries, hopes and joys. I hadn't mattered to any of them as I snapped their photos, but they took up space in my heart and in my imagination as each woman came alive on my paper. They mattered to me, because they mattered to God.

Every Sunday evening I attended Bible Study at the Frost's home along with ICS majors and others interested in missions. I made some good friends at this gathering. Their stories interested me, as did their desire to serve Christ cross-culturally. I was shy and mostly listened, but those discussions made a deep impression on me.

One night I talked to mom, probably in tears, because I was so unhappy despite doing the art I loved. I wanted to encourage disabled people and their families in India and everywhere. I felt so strongly that it was important for Christians to show people that God is good all the time, to all of us, and that everyone's life has beauty and possibilities. Mom listened and comforted me, offering a few ideas as I struggled with this. She also suggested that I seek counsel from Jim and Emily as well as others whose wisdom I trusted.

Naturally, given all I said to him, Dr. Frost encouraged me to take his first course in Intercultural Studies during the fall of 2008. There was no pressure. I knew I couldn't do more than that, and he didn't ask me to. But he thought it would offer me some perspective on cross-cultural ministry, some beginning cross-cultural skills, plus an opportunity to explore my sense of direction. He was right. Global and Cultural Awareness turned out to be one of the most important classes I have ever taken.

In August, I found myself at SBU again, in class with some of my friends from the Sunday night Bible Study. We learned to pay attention to cultural distinctives, to watch carefully and to listen to what meanings those differences might have. We tried to listen to everything without judgment about the "rightness" or "wrongness" of different cultural patterns and expectations, which is a lot more difficult than it sounds. Dr. Frost told us that to enter any new culture successfully, we had to come with the openness of a small child – ignorant, curious, willing to be corrected, playful, interested in everything, and eager to learn how to talk and to walk. He urged us to step back from our own cultural preconceptions and begin to see a new culture as its members do. Harder yet, he wanted us to try to perceive ourselves the way they do.

"Students," Dr. Frost used to say, "It is very important that you enter a new culture the way Jesus entered the world, as an infant, having to learn everything, dependent on others to show Him what it meant to be part of the community." He told us that if we weren't willing to follow that example, we were setting ourselves up for failure and disappointment before we ever began.

We divided into groups and Dr. Frost sent us out to immerse ourselves in an actual culture different from our own. We have a large Romanian community in Bolivar that interested me, but since most students were interested in Asia, I joined a group who chose to meet with Koreans in Springfield. It was a good lesson for me. I was used to doing, exploring, or reading pretty much whatever I wanted to by myself. But I was learning how much it matters to be flexible, to let go of my own preferences for the sake of the group. That is a lesson I guess we never fully learn. At least, I still find it difficult!

I truly enjoyed exploring Korean culture as it is still lived in Springfield. We worshipped in a Korean Church, which I loved because it reminded me of being in India, where I didn't understand any of the language but understood clearly the heart that praised God. The people of this congregation were friendly to us, gracious and eager to share their history, language and culture. The people served us a delicious meal and encouraged us to try new foods. A young person took us to local Asian shops where we purchased various small items and new foods to take back to share with the whole class. I developed a particular taste for Korean soda pop and even brought a bottle home. It remained in our refrigerator as a silent testimony to my commitment, until after my eventual SBU graduation when I drank it in celebration!

I was grateful that Dr. Frost didn't make a bunch of exceptions for me. As a group we had to decide how I would get to wherever we were going, and what my role would be when we got there. I had to just get over being shy about needing people's help. Students folded up my manual wheelchair and threw it into the trunk of a car, pushed me around, assisted me to the bathroom, and helped me back into the car. We worked it out. It was good to just do all this together with other students, and to complete a common project where my input was as necessary as anyone else's. In that group, my wheelchair was simply an inconvenience, not a big deal.

When the four of us attended Korean services, the church members asked questions about why I had no arms or legs. They expressed surprise that, disabled as I am, I was interested in missions. They were even more surprised that SBU faculty didn't discourage me to pursue this study. So, again, I was able to tell them about my life, about my time in India, and how I wanted to work cross-culturally with churches to encourage their disabled believers to participate fully in the church's ministry along with the rest of the congregation. In turn, the pastor encouraged me, saying he felt that God would bless many others through what I was being drawn to do.

As fall moved into winter, I realized I could probably take another class or two in the spring, and still manage to keep up. I had done well in the three classes I'd taken so far, so I signed up for three ICS classes, still with the understanding that I would never complete a degree. All I wanted was to learn what I could in my chosen area. I intended to use my art and my new cross-cultural skills to do my own cross-cultural work as the path opened up for me. Because my disability would certainly prevent me from working with any ordinary mission or non-governmental organization anyway, the degree seemed superfluous, expensive and time consuming, not to mention impossible for me to complete.

But registering for three classes instead of one turned out to be costly, too, so I applied for a Pell Grant to help with tuition. On the form, there was a box asking for confirmation that I was "working towards a degree." That hurt my conscience, since I wasn't. In fact, I even

105

asked some of my adult friends, teachers and mentors about this, whether it was even honest for me to say yes. If I did, I would get financial aid, if I didn't, I wouldn't. This represented a real ethical conflict for me. Of course, as one said, I was working toward a degree in the sense that I was taking the classes required for the ICS major; on the other hand, neither I nor anyone else thought that I would actually complete any degree. In the end I signed it, but not without a vague sense of guilt.

When the semester began, the late January weather proved challenging for me and my electric wheelchair. Fortunately, all my classes were in the Redford building, but I couldn't even get my wheelchair to school because of the deep drifts everywhere. We still lived out in the country, and hauling my little wheelchair trailer up icy dirt roads early in the morning after having pulled it out of freshly fallen snow was more than my mom could manage. I was afraid she'd have to stay on campus all day, just to get me from class to class by pushing my manual chair and carrying my stuff. Neither one of us liked that idea, but it seemed the best we could do.

Winter surely wouldn't last forever, but while it did, I expected to be stressed. The Redford secretary, Debbie Barnhouse, saw the problem immediately and decided to change the classes around so that all three of mine would meet in the same room. It did not occur to me then how many people this inconvenienced. I didn't think to ask which professors had "favorite" rooms they usually preferred for their classes. However, I sighed with relief when she told me.

Even after the spring thawed out the ground and relieved the pressure of transportation, that arrangement left me free to run up to the cafeteria with my electric wheelchair and a friend. It also allowed me to take myself to chapel without packing up, getting the book bag on the back of my chair, and then taking it back off an hour later, unpacking and hauling books and paper out again in another room.

Christian Doctrine was terrific, partly because I like theology, but mostly because discussing the Trinity, the meaning of salvation, or the significance of Scripture are just normal conversation topics at my mom's house. Everyone who shows up gets dragged into discussion if they stay around long enough. Storying and Discipling looked like fun, and I figured that wasn't going to be hard, either. I didn't know anything yet about World Christian Foundations, except that students who had taken it said it was the hardest class they had ever taken. But I was eager to begin.

It was natural to see the whole Bible as one great story, since that is how I learned it as a child. Therefore, communicating Bible events in chronological, natural story-forms made perfect sense to me. But it isn't easy for a foreigner to actually do it. The classroom exercises forced us to understand how thoroughly we would have to immerse ourselves in a new language if we really wanted to be able to tell God's story so that it would sound right and be compelling within a new cultural context. People like the Wycliffe Bible Translators face this difficulty every day, as do so many others who work for a long time to tell God's story in languages where it has never been told.

Can you imagine, for example, recounting the story of Jonah, while sitting out under desert stars where no one has ever seen or imagined a sea or a ship or even a big fish? Think how you might tell Jesus' parable of the Good Samaritan to people who had never even heard of Samaria, the Samaritans, Jerusalem, priests or Levites? And how would you talk about Jesus as the Lamb of God in the highlands of New Guinea, where people had never seen sheep, but definitely valued their pigs?

I was only beginning the ICS program as an ordinary girl, not expected to have all the answers. I was just walking one step at a time, enjoying the journey!

CHAPTER TWENTY

Crisis

With the spring semester over, I could draw and paint to my heart's content. Rivendell's beautiful flowers, the taste of ripe blackberries, and lazy afternoons on the porch with a glass of iced tea, rested and refreshed me. Life was full of the daily ordinariness that makes up so much of our life. And it was good.

Early in June, Dr. Stephanie Miller, Vice President for Enrollment Management at SBU (a position I didn't even know existed), called me to her office. Of course I was on my guard. I'd never met her, had no idea who on earth she was or what she wanted.

It turned out that Dr. Miller was Not Amused. I had wiggled through the institutional cracks, had somehow slipped under her radar, and had managed to take (and to make A's) in 17 hours of coursework without ever being enrolled for a degree. Well, of course not, I thought. I never intended to earn one. She told me in no uncertain terms that I could not just keep taking random classes at SBU, and that I needed to get serious about applying as a regular student. I was Not Amused, either. I had no desire whatever to do that. It was a stalemate – give in to institutional demands, or quit taking classes.

(I don't know how often this situation comes up, actually. Are there really that many people who go to university as non-degree students and take one or two classes at a time over several years? Are there enough to screw up the University's graduation rate? I doubted it.)

But as mom helped me into the car afterwards, I told her I wasn't going to do it. If they didn't want me, fine. I didn't care, anyway. I was furious. I was defensive, and definitely angry. I stopped to talk to Dr. Frost, but he, too, tried to convince me to work towards a degree. "You've done well in all the ICS courses you've taken. Why not come as a full time student? I really want to see you walk across the stage and receive your degree!"

My mom drove me away, saying nothing much, letting me argue and rage and justify my stubbornness. But underneath my own words I kept hearing what Dr. Frost had said. He thought I ought to do it. He assumed I could. For a few long minutes I fumed. But then it was over. I grabbed the cell phone and told Dr. Frost I would try. Mom was surprised, considering how resistant I had been two minutes before. So was I, as a matter of fact. But I had made up my mind.

When I told Dr. Miller, she tried to get me to back up and take the freshmen General Education classes in the fall. "No way," I retorted. "Dr. Frost said I could do this backwards and that's what I'm going to do. He's already registered me for my fall classes. I'll do all those others later."

She was still Not Amused, and commented that this was a Bad Idea. Still, I had given in to her pressure to enroll as a full-time, degree seeking student, so she began to help me figure out how to pay for this degree. I had already applied for the Pell Grant as a part-time student, so I had to go back and re-apply for full-time assistance. SBU offered me the Church Related Vocations scholarship. I applied for a Missouri Access Grant, and a scholarship from the Episcopal Church Women. Dr. Miller also encouraged me to begin applying for scholarships I had not realized were available. That was good advice because SBU has a lot of generous supporters who make scholarships available every year. In the end, thanks to the financial assistance I received, as well as the proceeds from selling my artwork, I graduated completely debt-free.

Dr. Frost always told his ICS students never to get into debt, because he knew We had struggle to pay it off in the years to come. If we actually completed this degree and accepted any cross-cultural ministry opportunity, we weren't going to be making big bucks, he reminded us. He even led a session for the entering freshmen every fall in which he warned them about the high cost of easily borrowed money. I still have the handout he gave me in the fall of 2008, long before I was enrolled for a degree. He wrote, "The borrower becomes the lender's slave," and, "Pray and get others to pray for what you need but cannot afford, such as money for school or ministry. If you someday will 'live by faith,' then begin now living by faith. Never borrow for ministry." I knew he was right. But I felt as worried as anybody else does who suddenly sees mounting bills and has no way to pay them. So I prayed.

And there were other complicating factors. For one thing, my electric wheelchair was dying. Not even my faithful mechanic at Bach Medical Supply could resuscitate it forever. Our request for a new one had been denied twice by Medicaid without explanation. The doctor sent off more paperwork, I applied yet a third time and waited. Without a reliable wheelchair, I couldn't go to school anyway, or do much of anything else, either.

For another thing, Vocational Rehabilitation, a source of educational funds for disabled people that Dr. Miller had suggested, couldn't help. An administrator scheduled me for an evaluation to see if I was eligible for financial aid, although it wasn't clear that there was any money available. In early July, a very young woman gave me several standardized, timed achievement tests in the middle of Bolivar's public library while people talked and milled around. I didn't expect to do well, and I scored poorly, especially on the math section. In the end, she determined I wasn't "capable" of college work, and tried to get me to opt for some other kind of simple job training for which Vocational Rehabilitation would pay.

I was discouraged, embarrassed, afraid, and full of doubt about myself, my abilities, and what I had agreed to do. I didn't see anything clearly, except Jesus. I didn't hear anything at all except, "Take the next step." But as summer dragged on, even that seemed impossible. I was an ordinary Christian facing some insurmountable difficulties, and I experienced every normal emotion. Sometimes people think that because I am a believer, I must have sailed through all these stresses calmly. No. For me, faith means hanging on to God no matter what, especially when everything in me screams, "Get out while you can!"

Worst of all, Dr. Frost met with me again in mid-July to say he had changed his mind. He agreed with Dr. Miller. The very day after I received my fall schedule in the mail, rich with the great classes I was eager to take, he announced that I would have to do as she said, begin back at the beginning, and take General Education classes instead. Oh, he was kind. He doesn't even know how not to be kind. But I had only agreed to do this stupid degree in the first place on the condition that I could finish the sequence of ICS classes with my friends first, and then do the other classes. I felt betrayed and coerced. Losing my classmates was especially difficult. We knew each other already. They were used to my wheelchair, and we prayed and hung out together at the ICS gatherings every week. Now they would forge ahead without me. Making friends with a whole new group of ICS students and joining their class mid-degree seemed formidable. There are never very many ICS majors each year, and they generally follow the whole sequence of classes together from beginning to graduation. They form a very tight group. Shy as I was, this completely undid me. I didn't think I could do it.

I spent the rest of the month moping around feeling miserable, wavering between tears and fury. On a lot of days, dropping out seemed like a good option, no matter what I had said earlier. I didn't have enough money to manage full-time tuition and fees even if I did decide to stay. Mom was concerned, anticipating another long winter of driving every day from Dunnegan to get me to school. I still didn't have a working wheelchair, and apparently I was too dumb for college level work anyway – "Not college material." That's what the Vocational Rehabilitation counselor had confidently declared to me and to Dr. Frost. As for the A's I'd already earned? Well, they were all in "Bible" and "religious subjects" so they didn't count. Obviously, they must have been easy classes if I had done well in them. That stung.

Later I found an email that my mom wrote to Emily. "Minda loves the Lord, and loves missions, and will find her own way to do it. I am not sure she'll turn around and agree, though, to do what we say she 'ought' to do, or in the way we think she should. I just don't know. It is hard to watch her struggle."

I took a week to visit Susan Easley and all her wonderful family. I needed to get away from SBU, from my art, from my mom, from the Frosts, from everyone else who Had An Opinion about what I should do. I wanted to swim in the pool, eat someone else's cooking, hang out with the girls, enjoy Brett and the boys, and just be with a sensible family. My dilemma over SBU wasn't even on their radar. I didn't need to talk about it. We could just relax.

But of course, I did tell Susan, and she listened. A few days later Susan emailed my mom. I didn't see this until many months later, but her note reflected my mom's concerns. "Cathy, are you sure Minda needs to be struggling so hard at college? You know she works three or four times harder than anyone else does. Do you realize she has no peers? She has 'friends' but they will always be able to do what she cannot. She will always be on the outside looking in, and wanting to be 'in.' No one there is really like her. She is struggling to be like the other students, but she will fail. And then she will feel as if it is her responsibility for failing. Let her find her own way. She will never be like them. I know she loves SBU, but does anyone there know what it takes out of her to do what she does? Is it worth it, Cathy?"

There were other summer stresses, too, that had nothing to do with me. A ferocious rain storm with damaging straight-line winds tore through Bolivar, causing serious damage to our church's roof. It destroyed the playground and soaked the carpeted sanctuary and classrooms. Mom, as the pastor of St. Alban's had plenty on her mind.

In early August after I returned home, Susan sent me a note that read, "You will find the path God has for you. He doesn't hide His will from those who seek Him earnestly." I knew those weren't just words.

On the afternoon of August 7, I sent a note to Dr. Frost that said, "I am going to go for it! Thank you for helping me see that maybe I can do it this way, even though I am very nervous about it, and about changing classes and losing my group. I want to keep Dr. Bayer's Old Testament class. Everyone says he is the best. And I want to keep the HIV-AIDs class. So go ahead and add Sociology, English Composition, and University Studies. It's going to be 13 hours, so that is really a lot for me, but I think I can do it."

Apparently, he didn't expect this turn-around. We had talked again that morning for a long time. I tried to make him see that I was scared, and felt both betrayed and manipulated by the system, even by him, since he had promised me one thing and then changed his mind. I told him how I felt like giving up and quitting school entirely. I didn't like feeling so trapped. But I think I felt free to say "yes" after he assured me that a "no" wouldn't affect the friendship mom and I valued so much with him and Emily. That freedom to choose mattered a lot to me. It was the only freedom I felt I had left.

I saved his quick response. "Minda, WOW! I'm not sure what all to say, but I do admire your grit and decisiveness! You were very well-prepared today, and I appreciate you communicating your concerns. I've registered you. I hope you have a great semester, and I'll see you every Sunday evening for Bible Study!"

Two weeks later I was in class. The congregation of St. Alban's had voted to replace the old roof with a beautiful, bright red one. My wheelchair had arrived and was working perfectly. My mom found the rest of the tuition money, and we were beginning to think about moving into town to make it easier for me to get to school. Everything Susan wrote was still true. My mom's anxieties were valid, but deep down I was happy and confident. If God had called me, and I believed He had, then God would make it possible whether I was "college material" or not.

I was humming that old hymn again. Christian faith is ordinary. I do not always find it easy, but it is always simple. "Trust and obey, for there's no other way, to be happy in Jesus, but to trust and obey."

CHAPTER TWENTY-ONE

Full Time, with Student ID

Only a few days after the semester began, I realized how wrong I had been to fight so hard against becoming a full-time student. Stubbornness and insecurity very nearly caused me to miss some amazing experiences. Dr. Bayer turned out to be an even better teacher than I'd expected; I dearly loved his lectures on the Old Testament. The HIV-AIDS class appealed to my practical imagination, so I stored away ideas I might use in the future. And although sociology wasn't difficult, it was engaging.

Surprisingly, English Composition turned out to be the most useful class of all, although it didn't begin that way. My first day in Todd Sukany's class presented me with a new challenge. I had never taken the ACT or the SAT, so I had no scores to offer as evidence that I could actually read and write. The English Department policy required students without those scores to take the remedial English class. Instead of going along with that decision, I decided to try to get the faculty to change their collective minds and make an exception. This time, I thought I was right to disagree. I knew I could write a complete paragraph even if I couldn't do math, so I sent an email to my teacher. Part of the email read, "Before class started today, you informed me that I might be in the wrong class because I have not taken the ACT or the English remedial class. I forgot to mention then that I have already taken 17 hours here at SBU, have made good grades and have done a lot of writing. I enjoy writing, and have not objected to writing even long papers. However, I do take a long time to complete them. I type one letter at a time with a ruler or a long pencil. In order to complete the in-class computer work for English Composition, I will need to come to the classroom early, return after my 12:30 class, or finish writing assignments at home and email them to you...I am determined to do this class to the best of my ability if you will give me a chance."

Within a day, a response from the English Department head appeared in my inbox – I could stay where I was and take the regular freshman English Composition class. I breathed a sigh of gratitude. Since the faculty had decided to give me grace, despite my strange academic history, it seemed only right to give that class my very best effort. I'm glad I did. Since I am slow to speak, and often think of what I want to contribute only after a discussion has moved on to another topic, writing offered me a way to communicate that seemed both effective and natural. When I was alone, I could take as much time as I needed to compose, edit, re-think, and begin again if I didn't like what I had written. Learning the discipline of composition also made for more thoughtful speech and gave me a better appreciation for the raw power of words. And soon I began to use them.

Once I wore the ID badge and drank SBU coffee, everything changed. Almost imperceptibly, SBU had become my school, and so I began noticing things I had mostly ignored before. It bothered me that there were so few disabled students on campus. Who was preparing disabled Christian teens in Missouri to live lives of significance in our world? At Camp Barnabas, I met many intelligent young adults who never even considered going to a university. I had been one of them. But now that I was on campus all day long, I discovered many reasons why I needed what SBU had to offer.

An English Composition assignment toward the end of September had me busy researching the SBU website and several others, all representing Christian colleges. I wanted to find out what potential students might see, and whether those schools were handicap accessible and welcoming to students with disabilities. Bolder than I had been a few months earlier when I was just a part-time student, I sent letters to the SBU Director of Web Services and set up a meeting to discuss why the SBU website showed no disabled students in casual group photos, although we had several students on campus in wheelchairs that semester. I wanted to know why there was nothing on our website to indicate any interest in recruiting or welcoming disabled students.

I even sent along some of my research, including this statement I found on the website for Calvin College – "The mission of Services to Students with Disabilities is to ensure that 1) otherwise qualified students are able to benefit from a distinctively Christian education based on the liberal arts, and 2) the Calvin community responds appropriately in a way that avoids handicapping the student with a disability." I loved that last bit: "…avoids handicapping the student with a disability." Someone understood me and others like me.

My note to our webmaster went on, "Isn't that wonderful? They even have a section titled, 'Will I be welcome?' For a disabled student that's a real question. The site itself is so positive, not just a list of what the disabled student must do to get adaptations he might need, but what the school sees that it must do to make the experience possible. Calvin College really portrays itself as a school that wants to include students with disabilities, because it identifies itself as a Christian school."

I found that the research for the persuasive essay that was intended as a standard assignment, and the interesting conversations I had with administrators, gave me as much pleasure as finally composing the essay. It didn't occur to me to wonder if the administrators who were so determined to make me a full-time student might come to regret their decision. I don't know if they ever did, but if my new sense of belonging increased my responsibility to represent SBU well, it also gave me freedom to campaign for change. Suddenly, I Had Opinions and I was learning how to express them.

University Seminar didn't require much work, and some of the material seemed painfully obvious, but I learned some things about myself I had not known before. We took the Myers-Briggs Type Indicator in class. At the time, I merely rolled my eyes, but when I saw the results I was surprised. I realized that I do what I do because I am who I am, with the kind of personality I was born to enjoy, to develop, to offer to God, and to use to serve others.

I recognized myself as an ISFJ right away. The test suggested that I

116

am an Introvert who really needs time alone in order to enjoy other people; a Sensing type, aware of things, both visual and emotional; someone who Feels, and acts from feelings rather than from ponderous thought; and a Judge, who likes analysis and a clear sense of what is right. It made sense to me.

It was kind of cool to see that I was part of another minority – only 7-10% of Americans fit this personality type. I wasn't nearly as rare or odd as I had feared. A great part of my personality didn't actually have anything to do with being disabled after all. Introvert became a beautiful word!

No one had ever suggested to me that I am "a nurturer who feels a strong sense of responsibility for others," or a "hard worker, detail-oriented, considerate of others' feelings, friendly and warm, and very conscientious," and that these traits would still have been true of me even if I had been born with arms and legs. It was a revelation of sorts.

It wasn't as unusual as I thought to "have a rich inner world that is not obvious to observers, constantly taking in information about people and situations that are personally important," and has "an excellent memory and perceptions that are often startlingly accurate." I used to think that I noticed everything because I was mostly confined to my wheel chair, watching and listening rather than participating in activities around me. Apparently not!

I was delighted to learn that ISFJs "learn best by doing, rather than by reading something in a book," and that, "more so than other types ISFJs are aware of their own internal feelings, as well as other people's feelings, but usually do not express them, or let on that they know how others are feeling." It was all so true. I discovered that my innate personality, not the fact that I am disabled, creates in me a "need for positive feedback from others," and "strong feelings of inadequacy" when under great stress. It certainly made those "down" moments easier to deal with; they don't mean anything terrible at all, and I don't need to take them so seriously. They're just part of how I am made.

I recognized that the most serious downside of this personality type was true for me, too. ISFJs tend to "hang on to negative feelings which may build up...until they turn to firm judgments against individuals, which are difficult to unseed once set." Everyone has their own unique areas of potential spiritual disaster, and this was definitely mine. When I prayed for God's strong help, it was usually for freedom to let hurtful things go as quickly as possible, and to forgive, whether the offense was directed at me or at someone else I cared about.

Seeing that I was simply a young woman with a particular personality type who also happens to be a committed Christian, solidified my sense of being ordinary, despite the less important, more visible fact that I am missing arms and legs. This was a delicious discovery. But typical of ISFJs, I never mentioned any of this to anyone.

Just for fun, I read a list of supposed ISFJs in history, and came up with Mother Teresa, Louisa May Alcott, Queen Elizabeth II, and Robert E. Lee, all individuals I admired. They had made something of their lives, so I figured God and I would make something of mine, too.

CHAPTER TWENTY-TWO

2010–Moving Along

I don't remember exactly why I was outside the Administration building that bitter winter morning, probably trying to deliver a check for tuition, but there I was alone. There was no accessible door opener so I couldn't get in, and there was nobody to open the door for me. I couldn't dig my cell phone out of my bag to try to call and ask someone inside to help, so I waited. The wind seemed to pierce right through my warm poncho, and my "hands" were freezing, even though I had my little arms tucked under it. People come and go all the time, so eventually I knew I'd find my way in, but I was miserable. Should I go and try to come back later? Keep waiting? I softly sang, "What a friend we have in Jesus," trying to make up my mind. A few minutes later, a big purple van drove by, slowed down and then stopped. I was surprised to see the University president, Dr. C. Pat Taylor, step down and come down the sidewalk to open the door! I don't think I'd ever spoken to him before, but there he was, on my side. I was just waiting for a door to be opened, but better than that, God opened up an opportunity for me to make a new friend. Dr. Taylor was a Very Important Person who stopped to do a little thing for a very ordinary student. He even did it cheerfully, although he had to have been as cold as I was. I never forgot that kindness. It was several years later that I found out it was really his wife, Judy, who first noticed me standing there and told Pat, "Get out and help her!"

It is true that the campus was not entirely accessible, but that is not the most important aspect of making a disabled student feel welcome. It's something else – an atmosphere, or perhaps an attitude more than the number of ramps or automatic door openers in the buildings. I felt that generous and friendly spirit at SBU from the first time I'd set wheel on campus on the way to speak to Dana Hacker's class as a shy teenager. Even handicap accessibility in a legal sense couldn't have helped me in situations that kindness alone could resolve. That's the accessibility that matters.

On a warm, sunny afternoon during spring, two friends walked along with me, all three of us laughing and chatting as we made our way down the hill towards the Redford building. The sidewalk was bumpy, but I was used to that so I didn't notice that the wheel on the right rear of my wheelchair was slowly coming loose. All of a sudden it popped off and went rolling away across the sidewalk and into the grass. Before I had a chance to react and be afraid of the chair falling over on its side, or of being thrown to the ground, a strong hand grabbed the chair and held it steady. I whirled around to see one of the SBU football players. He'd seen the wheel wobbling from a long way back, and had run to rescue me just in time, catching the chair exactly as the wheel came off. He noticed something wrong and responded immediately, before anyone else even realized there was a problem. He made my problem his business. Would that have happened on a large, busy campus? I am not so sure. Another student came outside, diagnosed the problem and offered to go buy the parts and repair it for me. I am certain that wouldn't have happened anywhere else. I don't know what their GPAs were. I don't know any of their struggles or successes, but I know their hearts. They were spontaneous in their concern. That was typical. That's the kind of heart I want, too – open, responsive and quick to get involved, even when an obvious need is not my problem.

I was signed up for pre-Algebra that semester. Everyone had to take a test to determine their math skill level. The University didn't really need to waste the paper on me. I knew where I belonged. Yet surprisingly, after seeing the results Dr. Bowling told me I could take College Algebra if I wanted, that I would probably do okay. I knew I had pushed my luck with Composition, and Algebra was terrifying to me in a way that Composition was not, even if I tested better than I had predicted. I stuck with pre-Algebra and was glad I did.

Sometimes I've found that it's wise to argue for more than we're offered – a more challenging class, an exciting opportunity, even a better salary. But sometimes it is smarter to admit unpreparedness, to acknowledge that we are up against a real mountain and not a mole hill, to hang back and work to make a foundation stronger before trying to build upon it. I was pretty sure taking College Algebra at this point would be trying to construct a building on a foundation of sand, and I had known better than that since kindergarten. "And the house on the sand went 'splat!"

Algebra was my personal nightmare. That's the biggest reason I had refused to consider completing a degree for so long. I knew perfectly well I couldn't pass it. There was no way. Math was incomprehensible to me, it always had been. For years I had struggled with numbers as they danced across the page. There was no way to type out math problems the way I can type a paper for English, so I struggled to write out problems by "hand." When I tried to copy them I lost numbers, skipped them, or gave up. I worked hard, but it seemed hopeless. So this class, even the remedial one, scared me to death.

When I entered the math lab that first day, my stomach was in knots. "Math anxiety" is easy to say and not too hard to recognize, but for the one who suffers from it, the anxiety represents an experience of sheer terror. Hesitantly, I found a place and looked around at my classmates. They all looked miserable. We were all "math failures" and everyone in the room knew we had to pass this non-credit class in order to get to the really impossible regular Algebra, for which we would get three hours of credit if we passed, and we would drop out if we didn't. The tension was palpable.

In a few minutes, a skinny man with a great smile on his face and gentleness in his voice entered the room and introduced himself. A minute later, Dr. Bowling specifically prayed that we would be encouraged. He prayed for himself, too, that he would be helpful and patient in his teaching. I'd never heard a teacher do that. He let God answer those prayers as day after long day he patiently explained the same problem or concept over and over, fifty times if that's what it took for the numbers to sit still and make sense. He had office hours in the math lab every day, and I went in to struggle with the problems every single day of the semester. He even gave us his home phone number and invited us to call if we got stuck. No matter how discouraged we felt, he would say over and over, "Keep your focus upwards." What wisdom! Math was terrifying, but God was not. Dr. Bowling once told me, "Struggle, but as you do, glorify God in the struggle." As long as I could remember that, as long as I could remember why I was pushing myself to understand a subject that was too hard for me, I was able to relax.

The next fall, I took College Algebra and was again in Dr. Bowling's class. I survived! I didn't make an A, but I was happy with a C. It's true that I didn't learn a lot of Algebra that I remember now. Rather, I learned a whole lot that was more important – to keep on keeping on when there is no end in view, to keep my focus upwards no matter what, and to "glorify God in the struggle."

When summer arrived, I took Biology, a four-hour science lab class. That was a bad idea to try to cram so much in such a short period of time. I had taken American Government during the short January term and thought it wasn't so awful. But the complex material in Biology included a lot of new concepts, vocabulary and processes to memorize. I found it to be extremely difficult to complete so much in such a short period of time. Nevertheless, I did it, tutored by my grandfather and two good friends from St. Alban's, both retired science teachers.

Finally, I could check another General Education class off my list. That's a lousy way to look at those classes, I understand. It is right to expect students to be at least somewhat familiar with subjects that intially hold no particular interest for them. That's what a liberal education is supposed to accomplish. In reality, I enjoyed learning. The coursework always caught and held my interest, but I was overwhelmed. I felt as if I were running to catch up all the time. I often felt as if I were simply marking classes off a list of hurdles I had to get over before I could get back on track and study what I wanted to learn.

During July, when the Biology class was complete, my friend, Marcy

Greenwade, drove to South Dakota to help me out during a two week trip to the Pine Ridge reservation. I had initially asked another girl to help, and paid her way to do it. But as I later discovered in Botswana, one of my greatest challenges will always be to evaluate a person's actual ability to handle my wheelchair and to assist me with personal care. Someone's initial enthusiasm doesn't always translate to actual willingness to do the work. The first week had hardly begun when the other girl gave up and found something else to do. Several hundred miles from home and unable to navigate without my electric wheelchair, that was hard. Marcy was amazing, though. Once she arrived, everything became easy.

Marcy is fun, for one thing. She has a genuine cross-cultural interest and lots of enthusiasm about learning new things. She could be quiet, too, spending time praying and reading Scripture with me without having to say a lot. Far from either abandoning me to do her own thing, or taking over a situation and telling me what she thought I ought to do, Marcy stood back and let me lead. For someone as competent and delightful as she is, this must have not always been easy, but it turned out to be important. Learning how to be both a companion and a "boss" to the same person is tricky. Marcy made it possible.

When I first arrived, the beauty of the reservation land consumed me. I spent a long time that first evening parked outside the Dream Center, just admiring the miles of empty prairie and empty sky that stretched to the horizon. I understood for the first time why my mom loves South Dakota. Those wide, open spaces are mesmerizing. I felt free there – free to dream, to pray and to breathe. Lori McAfee, who directs Wings as Eagles (WAE) ministries among the Lakota people of Pine Ridge, created the Dream Center as a safe space for children and families to spend time away from extreme poverty, violence and despair. I had arranged to spend this time working with her and learning from her ministry before pursuing the required six months abroad. My main objective was to watch, listen and absorb all I could. I wanted to understand the Lakota people, the circumstances and culture in which they live, the work being done by WAE, and then to serve the children in whatever ways I could, loving them with Christ's love.

123

My journal began, "After resting and meeting some of the other team members, I feel excited and anxious. I'm not sure what to expect for our journey into the small towns on the reservation, but I'm ready to take any challenge that comes my way. I pray to the Father that I may be an encouragement not only in my words, but in my actions as well."

The volunteers normally drove into one of the small towns every day, honked the horn and waited for kids to come running from houses all around. Lori generally made the rounds to half a dozen neighborhoods every week, bringing along the young volunteers from the Dream Center. The Lakota children were used to seeing the WAE van and knew there would be teenagers to play with, food, and often other treats as well. The kids loved the attention, grabbing the volunteers' hands as soon as they stepped out of the van. But when I got out, their initial reaction was fear. Children stood back, nervous and uneasy. I was used to that, and soon, with some encouragement, their natural curiosity overcame their reluctance. "What happened to you, Minda?" a little girl asked. Grinning, I replied, "I was born this way. God makes everyone different." It seemed to reassure her that nothing terrible had made me lose my legs and arms. Soon the little ones realized I could laugh and talk with them, even give hugs and work on crafts and play games. I was happy playing with the children, but it seemed like we did very little, especially as I became more aware of the desperate poverty so many of these children lived in, and the cultural disintegration that left them adrift.

The Pine Ridge poverty statistics are staggering. In 2005, the Department of the Interior reported unemployment at 89% in the reservation. There is almost no industry or commercial infrastructure on Pine Ridge to provide employment. The median income for a household is less than $20,000 a year. Infant mortality is the highest in the Americas, only minimally better than in Haiti. Approximately 60% of the homes on the reservation need to be burned and rebuilt due to the presence of dangerous black mold in the structures, but there is no funding to help the tribe do this. Many homes have no running water or electricity. According to the 2010 census, 51% of the population is age 24 or younger. The teen suicide rate is 150 times the national average. There are 18 gangs that roam the reservation, largely unopposed. Alcoholism and diabetes affect huge numbers of Pine Ridge's people. Life for many is overwhelmingly tragic. I felt that hopelessness and saw it in the eyes of the older teens who sometimes told us about their lives, but rarely about their hopes or dreams.

Towards the end of my time I journaled, "I got to speak to the children today, specifically about my life in a wheelchair. They have seen so much suffering, so much violence and terrible pain, so much death, that this wheelchair just seems like another 'thing,' another sadness, perhaps. But what did surprise them is that I am not sad for myself, only for them."

I so badly wanted them to believe that they can change their future; that God can use them to change life on the reservation. But how can they? Where will they find strength and courage, the money and the vision to do it? Faith does not change the circumstances in which these kids live and develop. Native American poverty is a national shame, and will require a national sense of urgency to change it. But faith can change a child's perspective.

Cole, a young Lakota boy who recently lost his best friend to suicide, wheeled me to the middle of the outdoor concrete basketball court at Evergreen, one of the small communities. Teens volunteering at the Dream Center and many Lakota kids gathered onto the court and formed a circle around me. As I began to speak, everyone fell silent. I just told them the simple story of my life. They seemed to listen as I described growing up disabled, and told them how I knew how rejection feels because I had also experienced it. I did not pretend anything. I told them about the love of God, not in a "pat" way, but because God's love had rescued me from despair about my future, and had given me joy in the midst of my suffering. I said that God could do that for them, too. I talked about how really good things sometimes happen even in the middle of hard times, and encouraged them to look for happiness and beauty in unexpected places and situations. It was simple. It was natural. I just wanted to show a future with hope, not to "fix" anything in the lives of these struggling young people. A Lakota teen walked over to me afterwards, all alone, and hugged me. "Thank you!" She said, "Thank you for saying that!" I pray she hears it over and over in her head as she makes her way into adulthood.

I came home from those two weeks with more questions than answers, more willingness to offer myself to be used by God than I had before, and with more awareness of my inability to change anything at all for the people I came to love. God's love does not fix things. There are Christians on that reservation whose lives do not include decent jobs, happy marriages or freedom from suffering. Knowing His presence and power does not magically remove anyone from poverty, hunger, disease or abuse.

The painful side of our American history matters more to the ones who were on the "losing" side of those cultural conflicts than to the "winners," who find it easy to forget what wrong has so often been done to people in the name of Christ. Black mold kills Christians as quickly as unbelievers, as does gang violence, alcoholism and heart disease. Christians and unbelievers alike are often helpless before these realities. Yet in every circumstance, God's powerful love and our hope in the future we do not yet see, are both stronger than we think. They may seem fragile, but can take root, grow strong, and bloom anywhere. It is our ordinary Christian privilege to bear witness to that truth with our lives.

Thy kingdom come, Thy will be done, on earth. In Pine Ridge. In Bolivar. In Botswana. In Syria and Palestine, in Somalia and Egypt, in Afghanistan and in Washington D.C. And mostly, in us, who know You, for the sake of those who do not.

CHAPTER TWENTY-THREE

Lead Me, Lord.
Lead Me in Thy Righteousness

By the fall of 2010, I didn't even hesitate to sign up for a full load of classes. Along with more general education courses, I was finally taking another ICS class, Spiritual Preparation, for the six months abroad with a group of students I barely knew. I was also eagerly anticipating Acting II.

Almost a year earlier, I had boldly stopped Dr. Sartwell in the hall to ask her if she'd ever let a disabled student audition for a part in an SBU play. "I don't see why not," she responded. "Well, then, I will," I thought to myself.

I loved theatre – live or televised, plays, operas, musicals – all of it. Perhaps it began when I was little and recited the lines I'd memorized from The Little Mermaid. Or maybe it started as I attended rehearsals for plays and performances at the University of New Mexico, especially when my sister, Becca, sang in the operas. Once we settled near Bolivar, my mom and I often attended SBU theatre performances and discussed them all the way back to Dunnegan, long before I ever stepped foot onto any other part of campus.

I really, really wanted to try it myself. So I took the first acting class and fell head over heels in love with the art of performance, and also with the often highly entertaining theatre students who populated that department. They were so "out there" compared to me, so interesting and creative. I loved hanging around them, soaking up the atmosphere.

Memorizing dialogue wasn't particularly hard, but letting myself do what a character would actually do, in order to help her get what she wanted, challenged me. The attempt pulled me out of my reserved nature and shoved me into the spotlight, swinging my "fist," yelling and screaming, teasing, flirting, whatever the character demanded of me. Dr. Sartwell kept telling me to get onto the floor in class and out of my wheelchair. She had some trouble persuading me to do it because I wanted to be at the same level as everybody else. I had too many memories of being a little girl staring at the knees of adults!

Acting became an exercise in understanding, in researching another person by trying to understand her goals, not self-consciously trying to meet my own. Each monologue required me to get inside a character's head as much as I could, rather than assuming I knew all there was to know about her the first time I read a script. It required me to figure out what she would do under the circumstances presented to me by the playwright. Acting provided a practical way to walk a mile in somebody else's shoes. I didn't always like my characters, but I came to see who they really were and to care about them.

It seems to me now that every Christian liberal arts student ought to take an acting class, along with another course I discovered a couple of years later, Cross-Cultural Communication. We generally assume that every reasonable person sees what we see, thinks the thoughts we think, values what we value, and does what we would do. It's not true, but making that assumption explains why we so easily misunderstand each other. Misunderstanding leads to wrong conclusions about what the other person or group is doing and why, which tends to divide people even more, even within families. Clearly it is true within our own country, as liberals and conservatives hurl accusations at each other without ever bothering to really understand what the other is trying to communicate.

Imagine how much more complex this becomes when people cross religious, linguistic, or cultural boundaries. Our world is shrinking. You don't have to go to China to find Mandarin-speaking neighbors, or to Africa to have a classmate from Ghana, or to Bangalore to discover a physician from India. They are here, and increasingly, we are also there. Many companies have international offices where Americans may be sent to live and work for months or years. The better people learn to understand each other, the better we will live together. And the better we do that, the better we will be able to proclaim the Gospel in ways that can be heard by others. Hearing the good news as really good news, is the first step towards the faith we hope that others will embrace – faith in Jesus, the Lord.

A good acting class might be the single best way for students to begin that process in a lived-out way, as an experiment, when it doesn't really matter to make mistakes. Before the semester ended, I had a couple of opportunities to practice what I'm preaching. I fumbled them, because I didn't even recognize that I was engaged in cross-cultural situations when they were right before my eyes.

Towards the end of October, the dean of students told me that a young woman in my summer Biology class complained that I had once asked her for help in the bathroom. She felt uncomfortable, but had not said anything to me. In fact, she cheerfully told me at the time that she was happy to do it. I was stunned. Normally during summer classes, I didn't need help anyway, since I wasn't on campus all day. Besides, I had made it a practice to ask specifically if someone was comfortable assisting me, and to make sure they knew it was okay to say "no."

When I expressed surprise and embarrassment, the dean tried to help me understand that "non-Christians might say 'no' when they are uncomfortable, but Christians always say 'yes' automatically, because they want to help, even when they don't want to do something." I commented that Christians are also supposed to be able to tell each other the truth in love! I didn't see this as a cross-cultural issue at the time, but it actually was.

When reflecting on this I wrote, "My feelings are not hurt when someone tells me she does not want to help me. But it makes me feel frightened and helpless when it seems as if my disability is being treated by some student as a problem for her. I have come to thank God for making me exactly as I am, but I do not feel very good about having to take the responsibility for resolving someone else's discomfort!"

In the end, the dean and I decided to ask each of my friends to sign a paper stating that they were willing to provide the very little help I needed. It worked, but the solution also created some new stress. What if I had an emergency and one of my pre-signed comrades wasn't available? For months I lived with that anxiety.

What I understood only much later is that the dean was right – Evangelicals do sometimes pretend to feel or think something we don't actually experience in order not to appear negative. Kindness is a Christian value. Sometimes people find it more authentically Christian to be at least "visibly" kind when they are uncomfortable, even if they also complain later. It may not be especially biblical to choose "niceness" over "truth in love" but it is pretty common among Christians. I had not considered that.

Another way Christians sometimes try to avoid negative feelings is to get God to declare what we don't dare say ourselves. During that same semester, an ICS student who was a potential, but clearly reluctant, partner for the upcoming six months abroad, announced publicly that God had told her she wasn't supposed to go with me. Apparently she, too, felt that expressing her real feelings would make her look bad and un-Christian, so she had to say that God had decreed her unwillingness to travel and live with me abroad. It was hard for me to relate to someone who used God as a cover for an attitude she clearly already had. No one can have any discussion after someone reports, "God told me..."

I wondered why she couldn't just say that she was afraid that my disability would slow her down, or interfere with her own freedom in another country. Why didn't she say that she didn't want to be burdened with me? It would have been more real to just say those things out loud. And perhaps, speaking the truth to each other in love, we would eventually have become friends, if not partners.

Only much later did I come to grasp the fact that many Christians, especially women, believe that being polite, avoiding conflict, being "nice," and never expressing negative emotions is what the Bible actually expects of believers. These two young women weren't being hypocritical after all, as I had thought. But their way of being Christian women clashed with mine, and left us both bruised.

I simply wasn't raised to understand Christianity that way. I expected other Christians to say what they meant and how they felt because my family, especially my mom, did. I wasn't used to trying to decode someone else's words or body language when what they said wasn't what they meant. I wasn't good at it. It wasn't my Christian cultural pattern of communication.

We were all believers, but we simply didn't understand each other at all, and all of us were unhappy.

If I had realized then that this was a cultural difference in communication, not the difference between the "right" way of handling problems and the "wrong" way of doing it, we might all have found easier ways to walk through this difficult semester. As it was, that fall semester of 2010 stressed me more than anything else ever did. I kept moving ahead, but with a huge weight in my heart, and often, tears just behind my eyelids.

It can be lonely enough to be a believer in an unbelieving world. It is also lonely when Christians are at odds with each other, neither quite understanding why. And it is harder yet when each is pretty sure the other is just being stubborn or deliberately difficult! I found it lonely that semester to beg God for patience, understanding, wisdom, and for the strength to just keep on keeping on, and to hear no word from the Lord at all.

This is one of the haunting, quiet choruses we often use at St. Alban's, especially during communion:

"Lead me, Lord. Lead me in Thy righteousness.

Make thy way plain before my face.

For it is thou, Lord, thou Lord only,

who makest me dwell in safety."

As the semester ended, I had no partner for my six months abroad, and no international placement willing to take a disabled ICS student. My acting class gave me joy, as did interacting every day with ordinary students who didn't know or care about any of my worries, but otherwise very little else did. Even prayer was darkness. I was more discouraged than ever.

Still, every time Kathy Brown played that little chorus, I cried. It was the prayer of my heart: "Lead me, Lord…in thy righteousness."

Part of what it meant for me to trust God then, was to keep walking in the dark, from security into insecurity, from the known into the unknown, from certainty into doubt, seeing nothing at all, still clinging to the Lord Jesus. It was all I could do.

CHAPTER TWENTY-FOUR

Spring Thaw

Just before our Christmas break, I wrote a letter to the people I had previously asked to be prayer partners with me as I prepared to go abroad. It was a class assignment to begin with, but rapidly became more than that. I had chosen only seven people, but each of them was someone I knew for sure would pray carefully, and each had been important to my Christian growth. They belonged to Baptist, Nazarene, Roman Catholic, Episcopal, Evangelical Free and Covenant churches. It wasn't planned like that. It just happened. Several of them had been my mother's friends before I was born, whose spiritual influence had affected our whole family. Only one was a student, Sarah Bottorff, a Biblical Studies major who plans to complete a Master's degree and work as a Christian counselor. My best friend at SBU, she and I often talked and prayed together. I knew I could count on her.

Despite the stresses of the fall semester, my letter was hopeful, grateful, and even optimistic about the future I could not see. I wrote, "I have taken every Saturday morning this semester to do a personal prayer retreat. I usually select a passage from Scripture and read it over a few times. Then I think about what it means, pray about my response to it, and journal. Most of what I have written is a confession. God uses Scripture to show me my own sins and failings and weaknesses, and yet I also see how much my Father loves and encourages me. I remember how great He is, and God reminds me of my own deepest desires, too – how much I want to serve and honor Him for all my life."

I had decided that the likelihood of finding a partner who wanted to go abroad with me, and was actually free to do it, was going to be slim. So I made up my mind to go alone and find "partners" and friends wherever I landed.

Instead of traveling overseas alone, Dr. Frost suggested I look into a stateside placement, perhaps on one of the Native American reservations or in an urban immigrant community. I wasn't ready to accept this accommodation until I had exhausted every possibility for doing what everyone else was expected to do. I didn't like setting this precedent for one thing. I was still hoping that other young people with disabilities would hear a call to serve God cross-culturally, and I wanted to somehow be the pioneer for them and for SBU. I researched every situation I could think of and during Christmas break I wrote letters like mad to friends, agencies, and anyone who might know some potential placement for me. But every possibility evaporated almost as soon as it was suggested.

"When the Lord closes a door, somewhere He opens a window." I was only a little girl when I first heard and memorized this remark made by the Abbess to Postulant Maria at a critical point in the musical The Sound of Music. I believed it. I still do.

So I got ready to enjoy the winter break with my family, including Becca's charming thirteen-year-old, Marcus, her little ones, Sarah and Bobby, plus her newest foster baby, an enchanting six-month-old named Elijah. For a few days, I forgot all about the struggles that had seemed so overwhelming only a few weeks earlier.

The last days of Advent sped by, and soon it was the silent night, Christmas Eve. Our darkened church was full of quiet candlelight and carols. "O come, all ye faithful, come let us adore him," the organ sang. We read the ancient words of Jesus' birth, and Becca sat in the back rocking her new baby, bending over him as tenderly as Mary leaned over the infant Jesus. In the midst of all that wonder, I realized I had stopped trying to shove that stubborn door open. Instead, I was keeping an eye out for some window I hadn't yet noticed.

One of my prayer partners, Marian Goble, worked for many years as a medical doctor with chronic drug-resistant tuberculosis patients.

More importantly, she has lived her long life in deep trust and faithful love. My mom was about my age when she decided to make Marian her friend. It was a good choice. For all these years, Marian has been a wise counselor and teacher – the woman everyone depends on to be steady and gracious with the gentleness of Christ. She is the most important of my many grandmothers. Marian understood how worried I was, but she never offered anything remotely resembling sympathy.

During January she wrote, "I find that my times of greatest satisfaction (and I believe of greatest effectiveness) are preceded with times of quietness before God. You are at the beginning of life, Minda. May God give you grace to discern His will, as you quietly seek Him, and actively prepare yourself to serve in His chosen way." Quietly. Without saying so, Marian sensed my nervousness and the anxiety that gnawed at my spirit, and quieted it by simply reminding me that I would know better what God wanted me to do if I stopped and rested in God's strength.

Survival Abroad, the final ICS course before going abroad, was soon in full swing. I plunged in enthusiastically. Eventually, Dr. Frost began to encourage the rest of the faculty to let me try to go abroad alone (contrary to department policy) if I could locate a place willing to have me. For a long while I thought it might be Haiti because my mom had so many friends there. The only large school for disabled children in Haiti, St. Vincent's, has been operated by the Episcopal Church for many years. That seemed like an obvious place for me to consider. My mom also had friends at the Baptist Mission in Fermathe, where a small hospital and many rural schools and churches serve the needs of mountain people. A couple of orphanages, one operated by Haitian Roman Catholic sisters and the other directed by Pentecostal Americans, were possibilities as well. Perhaps I could work at Schweitzer Hospital near Becca's birthplace in the Artibonite Valley? And what about Grace Children's Hospital, an inter-denominational hospital for children with tuberculosis where my mom had once worked as a volunteer? I contacted them all.

But as it turned out, even the institutions most willing to have me

135

come, urged me not to try to get to Haiti yet, because so much of what was destroyed during the January, 2010 earthquake had not yet been rebuilt. One of the young priests at St. Vincent's wrote me in March and said, "We are working on getting everything ready for you to come. As soon as the situation is getting better, we will let you know. The principal of the school also sees your presence in two ways. He says you can be good for the children and the parents. He also says they will teach Creole language and culture to you. But as I told the bishop, the situation at St. Vincent's is really critical. The building is not secure, dust and rubble are all around us, and we have moved the children to the country for now. We can't finish all of the building yet. We care for your safety. I am eagerly awaiting you. Maybe it will be December." Similar answers came from our other friends. Quietly, I stepped back to see what God would do.

An orphanage in Guatemala offered me a place at Casa Bernabe, where other SBU students sometimes traveled for short-term mission trips. But when the missions' office investigated that option closely, we discovered that the building was large and spread out over three levels, with steep stairs and no elevator. The director thought I would be great for the kids and was willing to work with me, but that housing situation wasn't going to work, even with assistance. So again, I tried to simply, quietly, let it go.

I kept remembering Marian's words and continued my Saturday morning prayer retreats all spring. I needed silence, so I looked for it. Going to Africa was my deepest heart's desire, for reasons I didn't even understand. But I couldn't see any way to do it. So in the midst of school assignments and my own disappointment, I tried to keep myself quiet before the Lord so that I could see, day to day, whatever He showed me.

None of it was easy. Everyone else talked excitedly about their partners and placements, the languages they would be learning and the opportunities that continued to open for them. My picture was on the printed prayer cards, right alongside theirs, for the June through December six months abroad experience. But it seemed increasingly likely that I wouldn't be going anywhere.

136

Still, I kept on with each next thing. For me, that included coping with February snow (all 22 inches of it!), which left my electric chair grounded and me back in the manual chair for a week. It was grim. No matter who volunteered to do it, shoving those wheels through snow and ice was difficult for my friends and occasionally even dangerous for them, as they slipped and slid across campus. It gave me fresh appreciation for their kindness, and also for my electric chair, recognizing how few disabled persons in our world ever have access to this kind of technology. It also meant doing homework for World Religions, The Baptist Denomination, and Fundamentals of Speech. I had another theatre class and, of course, Survival Abroad. It was ordinary now for me to carry fifteen hours. I knew I'd come a long way from the days when taking even a couple of classes at a time seemed scary to me. I had learned a lot about managing my time, organizing my work and planning ahead to meet deadlines.

Later that spring, Marian sent me a couple of verses to think about, one of which was Luke 1:8-11: "Once when Zechariah's division was on duty, and he was serving as priest before God, he was chosen by lot, according to the custom of the priesthood, to go into the temple of the Lord and burn incense. And when the time for the burning of the incense came, all the worshippers were praying outside. Then an angel of the Lord appeared to him, standing at the right side of the altar of incense." Along with the verse, she wrote, "Sometimes when we are simply doing our religious duties as we are supposed to be doing, praying, worshipping, or studying Scripture, the Lord shows up and speaks when we least expect it. What seems ordinary can suddenly become full of life." She just kept nudging me to do the ordinary stuff of daily life, to wait and to trust. She didn't preach, but she was firm and insistent. And wise.

When spring finally arrived, my heart thawed, too, and my natural optimism began to resurface. Mom drove me to Nebraska, where someone had invited me to show my art in order to sell the paintings and drawings to continue raising money for my six months abroad. I can hear the note of hopefulness in my prayer letter, "Pray for me to be able to show the beauty of God and His goodness to others. I am very excited, not only to share my art, but also my testimony with a group of women who have been very supportive of my call to missions."

A couple of those women were actually my mom's high school classmates, who did a great deal of planning in order to make my trip successful. Once again, I discovered that when two or three are gathered together in His name, age doesn't matter, denominational affiliation is irrelevant, and Jesus really is present, alive and glad to be among us! That never ceases to amaze and delight me. I returned with more than a thousand dollars to add to my growing ICS account.

I loved interacting with the people who came to see my watercolors and ink drawings. At one event I noticed a little boy, maybe five or six-years-old, who loved a bright abstract painting called The Heart of God. I kept watching him go back to that piece over and over, and heard his comments to his mother about how it "looked like God." He was so sweet and sensitive. We talked some, just the two of us, and after returning home, I sent him a personal note. So many adults have encouraged me by listening, and I wanted to let him know that I had heard his heart, too.

Every time someone came up to me and thanked me, or told me how moved or inspired they were by my art, or my perseverance in school, or my desire to serve God cross-culturally, I felt God's pleasure. I knew I was doing what He wanted me to do. Once again, God showed me that art and the blessing of my disability go hand in hand, both evidences of God's love for me – and for others.

During June I wrote, "My classmates are all leaving for their six months abroad this week. I am praying for them, and glad for them, but it is kind of hard not to be going, too. Sometimes I find myself getting very impatient because I just want to get up and go, but I know that an impatient way just doesn't work." The letter ended, "I am glad to report that I now have all the funds required for my six months abroad safely in the SBU account! I had determined not to beg, and I haven't, but not because I am embarrassed to ask. I think it is fine to ask people for financial help, but this time I just wanted to let God show me that He would provide for me if He wanted me to go. Of course, I sold a lot of artwork, but many people gave me money I didn't expect. Sometimes it came from complete strangers. I wanted to see what God would do for me if I did what I could do – and what He did is bigger and better than I ever dreamed!"

However, I still had no place to go. What did this mean? It meant that my way was still clear—trust and obey. Be quiet. Wait. Prepare.

CHAPTER TWENTY-FIVE

Changes

As soon as finals were over, I made an appointment with my doctor, Lori Cohen, to talk about an elective hysterectomy. I already knew that bearing children would be extraordinarily difficult and even dangerous for me. My periods were heavy, irregular and hard to manage. In the States, I used continuous birth control to keep my periods away, but what if I couldn't find something in my new home that worked as well as what I bought here? What if I lost the pills, they were stolen, or if I simply ran out? Besides, in case of the rare possibility of rape, here or anywhere in the world, I didn't want to risk becoming pregnant just to agonize over how to cope with that.

She agreed that hysterectomy was reasonable, despite my youth, but finding a surgeon willing to do it turned out to be surprisingly difficult. Living in a body like mine, it's hard to imagine any other way of being, so I didn't see the problem. But normal people have arms for IV access, and for the measurement and regulation of blood pressure, both of which are necessary when a surgeon operates. I don't, so no one wanted to touch me. The liability, as well as the obvious difficulty of simply figuring out how to do this surgery, held them back.

One well-respected gynecologist refused outright, citing the risks. When I appealed to her faith, describing just how much difference this would make for me when I went to serve in a cross-cultural setting, she simply said, "Then you need to change your goals." Her words were a cold reminder of what I already half-feared, that sooner or later even my strongest supporters and professors at SBU would turn and say the same thing to me.

In fact, Dr. Sartwell had already come up with a contingency plan. In case I didn't get to go abroad, she said that I could complete another major, Speech Communication/Theatre, and graduate at the same time I was already anticipating completion of my degree. I'd done enough theatre classes already to be well on my way to that degree. When I looked ahead to the fall semester, I went ahead and declared that second major. It met my needs and interests, and gave me a solid back-up in case I couldn't complete the ICS major.

Dr. Cohen called several surgeons trying to find one who wouldn't automatically say "no." We needed someone with the courage to take a risk since I was willing to take the largest risk. I needed someone who could problem-solve quickly if necessary. And I wanted a Christian doctor, someone who would understand me and not suggest that I just ignore what I sensed to be a clear calling. That's a lot to ask.

Finally, Lori phoned me with good news. She had asked Dr. Thomas Shultz to consider doing the surgery and he hadn't seemed afraid to try. The first time we met, I began explaining my situation, and smiling, he cut me short. "You're twenty-three years old, and you know what you want." As I began to tell him about my ICS major, and why this surgery was important to me, he looked up and said matter-of-factly, "Inter-Cultural Studies – that's missions, right?"

Within about three minutes, I was sure this was the man I wanted to do the surgery. Now if only he would agree. I am so grateful to be living in this century. Not very many years ago the concept of robotic surgery didn't even exist, except in someone's imagination. Now a surgery as extensive as a hysterectomy can be done (normally on an outpatient basis) using this technique. It sounded a little like science fiction! Before I left Dr. Schultz's office, he had scheduled the surgery for July 22. He thought he could get an arterial line in my groin to measure blood pressure, and use the large vein in my neck for IV fluids. I felt as if I were rolling on cloud nine when we emerged into the summer sunshine.

A couple of weeks later, the nurse called me back to the pre-op area. I could see that the anesthesiologist wasn't quite as confident as the surgeon had been, but he started the IV in my neck and tried to speak hopefully about getting femoral artery access once I was in the operating room. Soon mom and Emily took themselves to the waiting room to begin their vigil.

It shouldn't have been a long one, but as time dragged on with no word, mom sensed trouble. Finally, Dr. Schultz emerged, looking anxious. No one had been able to get a line into the femoral artery he knew was there, and I'd been under anesthesia, essentially unmonitored, for a long time already. He was going to call a cardio-thoracic surgeon to try, but if he couldn't get the line in, the surgery would have to be aborted.

Mom and Emily prayed. They paced, thumbed through old waiting room magazines, and waited. When Dr. Schultz came out next, he was triumphant! They'd gotten the arterial line in, had done the surgery, and were just waiting for me to wake up. When I did, I was immediately wide awake, not even groggy. All I asked was, "Did you do it?"

I recovered quickly and was ready to begin class in August, grateful and happy to have this surgery behind me. I was also grateful for a surgeon who not only met all of my "requirements," but treated me with generosity and abounding kindness. God orchestrated it all rather well, after all! How much easier our lives would be if we only trusted Him more.

On the very first day of public school, Becca got a desperate call from the foster care worker with whom she usually worked. After removing little Elijah from Becca's home in June to send him to another foster home where his sister and little brother lived, the worker suddenly wanted Becca to take all three children "temporarily." Before many weeks went by, the placement became permanent. Becca now had first-grader, Olivia, just a year older than her kindergarten-age sister Sarah, three-year-old Xavier and his little brother, Elijah, plus severely developmentally delayed Bobby, who was eight. Marcus, of course, was ecstatic! He loves kids and could hardly wait to begin teaching the little boys soccer and wrestling. It was all good. But it also meant that my mom had to help Becca move yet again, this time into an old house on a huge lot, where there were enough bedrooms and plenty of space for the children to play.

At the same time, my grandma's oncologist discovered a new cancer, this time in her liver. She'd coped with breast cancer for years, but this news crushed her. She knew what it meant, and became depressed and angry.

So as classes began for me that semester, my mom spread her time between our Bolivar duplex, Becca's house, and my grandparents' home, trying to help us all. I decided to cheer her up by reporting nearly everything Dr. Reeves said in Early Pauline Epistles. She had already read the textbook, and since she definitely "privileges Paul," I was pretty sure she would hear about that than anything else that was going on at school! Every evening, while my mom cared for Grandma in one room, my grandpa sat with me at the kitchen table. He explained meteorological concepts while happily eating ice cream and urging it on me.

Before we had gotten very far into the semester, I received the best possible news – the Anglican bishop of Botswana, Trevor Mwamba, was willing to have me come to his diocese in southern Africa. He even suggested an appropriate supervisor, Dr. James Amanze, professor of Christianity at the University of Botswana and an Anglican priest. I could hardly believe it! My friend Sandra Zarins, who volunteered with the church in Botswana, suggested that I might share her first floor flat in Gabarone. I could hire a woman to help and do my service project at St. Peter's, a large day care center for orphaned and vulnerable children in the nearby village of Mogoditshane. Sandra even had internet service, important for sending assignments back to SBU! After months of uncertainty, everything quickly fell into place, exactly as Marian had predicted. When I was busy doing the most ordinary things, reading Scripture day by day, meditating in quiet, all while struggling to understand the science of weather, God showed up.

Late in October, my grandma died peacefully at home. Becca's children were beginning to settle into their new home, and I had purchased my tickets for an early January departure, when Sandra could fly back with me to Botswana. Had I not already been prepared spiritually, financially, academically and practically when that incredible call came, I'd have missed the best six months of my life.

CHAPTER TWENTY-SIX

Bless the Lord, O My Soul

Baka Moreno, mowa we me le tsotlhe tse di mo teng ga me, bakang Liena la gagwe le le boishepo. Dipesalome 103:1

Botswana, at last! The plane touched down in Gabarone, and my first glimpse of Botswana revealed happy faces of Christians who came to welcome me. If I had been tired before, I wasn't any longer. I was so happy to finally be in Africa, that I couldn't stop singing.

At St. Peter's Daycare in Botswana

"Bless the Lord, O my soul, and all that is within me, bless his holy name" (Psalm 103:1) came to mind often during those first few days. All I wanted to do was to praise Him for His faithfulness to me. I was enchanted with everything and everyone I met, the beauty of the land, even the summer heat, which I loved coming from freezing cold Missouri. I could hardly believe I was there after so many delays and frustrations. I woke up smiling and went to bed grinning. The language was beautiful, even if incomprehensible. My flat-mate made me welcome in so many different ways, and the monkeys, running across the clothesline and chattering outside my window, made me laugh. Immediately, it seemed, I felt at home, as if I had finally landed where I belonged. It was a feeling that I never lost, not once in those six months. No matter what I encountered in those many weeks, Botswana was home, and I loved it.

I encountered stressful situations that stretched me, pushed me to my limits (and sometimes beyond them!), luring me into deeper trust in the Lord who had made this way plain and led me every step of the way. Early on, for example, I had to hire someone to assist me with basic shopping, some personal care, and getting me to wherever I needed to be since I had brought only my manual wheelchair. I was less independent in Botswana than I am at home, but since the country is not yet very wheelchair accessible, I needed to be practical and count on the manual chair to be adequate.

It didn't take me long to recognize that I didn't have any idea how to interview someone from a different culture, in a different language, or how to explain in ways she would understand what I needed her to do, even with a good interpreter. I had very little idea how to choose between several candidates who wanted to work for me. Sometimes my intuition was wrong and someone had to be replaced. Nevertheless, my helpers and I muddled through, had some incredibly wonderful times together, as well as a few miserably difficult ones. Not until I was nearly ready to come home did I begin to understand what I ought to have done differently, how I should have behaved with a local employee, and how I could have made myself more clear in a culture where I must have been seen as hopelessly impolite. It was all part of my cross-cultural journey, a normal part of being both "at home" and also a "stranger in a strange land." I felt like a little child learning everything for the first time, and daily I grew up a little more.

All the while, I had to settle into my new life as an American college student – to haul out my computer, organize my time and my work space so that I could complete ICS class assignments, begin learning Setswana, and decide on the specifics of my service project. I had to figure out how to manage laundry, prepare food, purchase a local cell phone, call for a taxi to take me to any appointments I made (since I couldn't get up into the much cheaper bus), and live comfortably on African time. That was all easier than I anticipated. It was strange to be simultaneously more academically and socially independent than I had ever been without Bolivar friends, family or professors nearby, and at the same time, so heavily dependent on other people to teach me the simplest words and proper Motswana behavior.

My assistant, Ntebeleng, got used to pushing me up the little road we lived on, and then across a very busy street to get to SPAR grocery store. We had to make this trek every few days since I couldn't haul much in the bag attached to my wheelchair, and she couldn't carry anything at all while pushing me. She began teaching me Setswana, correcting my pronunciation, and insisting that I speak both correctly and politely by Botswana standards on our walks away from home.

Little by little, I realized I could carry on short conversations, pick out familiar faces in a crowd, ask for items and pay my grocery bill myself, and even understand some of what was being said (or sung) in church. New foods, new smells, new greetings – everything around me was different, and yet more strangely familiar than even India had been. This was a constant surprise and a daily joy. I didn't understand it, but I embraced the ordinariness of my daily life in Gabarone with enthusiasm.

Every few days my supervisor, the Rev. James Amanze, Professor of Theology at the University of Botswana who is also an Anglican priest, came by the flat to check on me, to offer wisdom, encouragement, advice, prayer and generous doses of laughter. He worked with me to determine which local group of people would be most accessible for my ethnographic research, and suggested ways to approach my studies. He also urged me to get to know the college-age youth of the Diocese and participate in their activities. He then set me free to do whatever seemed best to me, repeatedly telling me to seek new opportunities and possibilities, and to pursue them as they arose. I took that advice seriously.

A few weeks after arriving, my helper and I went to St. Peter's Day Care Centre for orphaned and vulnerable children to talk about my several-days-a-week service project. Gladys Mudereri, a nurse, directs the Centre with abundant grace and firmness; I loved her immediately. Her husband, Andrew, is the priest in charge of St. Peter's parish, which consists not only of the congregation in Mogoditshane where the Day Care is located, but five other churches as well. Both of them are amazing, positive, hopeful people whose personal cross-cultural experience gave them insight into my own. Born in near-by Zimbabwe, the Mudereri's had come to serve in Botswana twenty years before and stayed. They raised their children, became fluent in Setswana, and took Botswana citizenship. It can't have been easy to set aside their own culture, language and people, even if God had sent them to Botswana, but they did.

That first morning, Gladys took us into the dining hall where the children were finishing up their breakfast. When Ntebeleng and I entered the room everyone became silent. Obviously I was a curiosity for them as I had been in India and in Pine Ridge, and at first, even in my Bolivar neighborhood. It wasn't many days before those same shy children ran to me, held my hands, pushed me around, and tried to teach me Setswana names for things, all while more or less oblivious to the wheelchair or my missing limbs. They became my own beloved children as I got down on the floor with them, read them Bible stories in my heavily accented Setswana, as well as in American-accented English. I helped them to act out the stories, wrote simple English lines, gathered up costumes and even found props. I bought fish sticks and bread to bring along when the children reenacted the story of Jesus feeding thousands of men, women and children with only the gift of a little boy's lunch. No matter which story we acted out, the children were unfailingly charming. They knew exactly what to say and do, and

147

played their roles as if they participated in theatre every day.

The children performed the Passion Play for their parents during chapel the week before Easter. The children we selected for the major parts carried off their performance perfectly. "Jesus" seemed entirely believable in his role, as did the soldiers and the disciples. The little girl, who had been selected to be the maid, shook her finger in "Peter's" face and accused him so forcefully of having been with Jesus, despite his denials, that "Peter" burst into tears! I loved every bit of every day I spent with those children.

Gladys approved of this disruption because she agreed that learning to re-tell and act out the stories could help the children develop their understanding of God's love for them, and also help them learn English. Knowing some English is very important even for little children as they prepare for public school in a country where English is widely spoken and commonly used in textbooks and upper level courses.

We also visited the Cheshire Center for disabled school-age children so I could begin to see what is being provided for them. On my first visit I was able to hold several of the most severely disabled. I saw God's face shining through each precious little person. I wondered how their families were coping, and whether they had any encouragement as they dealt with the stresses their children's disabilities presented. One little ten-year-old, Kaleboga, could not move her legs, and both hands were twisted so that she could not easily grasp anything. I held onto her for a long time as she tried to reach out to me. I will never forget her radiant smile. We simply sat there awhile, quiet in each other's embrace. I came across another little boy whose disability was similar to Kaleboga's, but he was older and slightly more mobile. He wanted to take pictures of me with him and continuously asked Ntebeleng to "flash some snaps!" At least the children weren't shy! The Director arranged for me to do some volunteer work there, and invited me to participate in their February fund-raising walk in Gabarone.

My schedule began to fill up with visits to various schools to talk about my life, and how God's love gives hope and vision to all of us. I talked to people from several denominations about the need of the whole Church to include disabled persons in their work, not only as objects of ministry, but as participants in it. My young friends drove me repeatedly to Tlokweng, a nearby village where I was doing my ethnographic research. In between other activities, I decided to organize a couple of art shows so that disabled persons could demonstrate and sell their art. Everything I did and the people I met along the way led to more invitations and possibilities. In the evenings I studied late, read all I could find about my new home and people, drank cup after cup of delicious tea, and slept contentedly.

One afternoon I got a call from a physician at Princess Marina Hospital, asking if I would come and encourage a young woman who had recently lost her limbs to an infection. Of course I could! The next day I rolled in to meet Maleboga, a young mother in her thirties. My Setswana wasn't very good, and her English was also halting, but we became instant friends. The nurses told me she couldn't feed herself, hold a cup, or dress herself at all. "Oh, no," I thought, "This ends now." I asked the nurses to bring her dinner with an extra fork. I began to show her how to catch her food and keep it on the fork as she put the handle down on the edge of the plate, while tilting the tines upwards with her stump so that she could bend over and take a bite. We practiced holding and lifting the coke she loved. Before the meal was finished, Maleboga was feeding herself triumphantly! We were both

Maleboga and me

149

proud. That incident initiated a collaborative friendship that didn't end until I had to return to the States.

Over the weeks we had together, she discovered ways to do everything, just as I had done as a child. When I saw her beginning to draw and to write her story in careful English, my heart swelled with pride in her ability and her courage to keep working towards independence. Before I left, we had traveled in a taxi together and eaten out in a restaurant in public, which she handled with grace although the idea of being "seen" had been so frightening to her. I had even taken her to visit the children at the Day Care Centre, where the little ones greeted her as easily and politely as they welcomed me every day. To see that the children weren't frightened by her appearance gave her hope that she'd be able to go back to her town and parent her own girls, even though she will obviously need the same physical assistance I do.

She realized slowly that what I said was true – she had lost only her arms and legs, not her mind, her beauty, her strength or her determination. She was still a whole, real person, as she had been before. Nurses, physical therapists and young physicians were curious about both of us, and so together we spoke to a gathering of medical personnel, showing what we can do. We even urged the professionals to let disabled people teach them how to help us!

I think she came to enjoy showing off her new abilities, especially as people seemed to take her seriously, to respect her, and to see her as "ordinary," only missing a few body parts. One afternoon, Dr. Amanze came to see how we were doing. He was so startled and impressed that he exclaimed, "We need to start a school! A 'Minda' school to teach people how to cope with disabilities." It made perfect sense. My imagination went to work right then and there. Why not create a space where disabled persons, who have found ways to handle their limitations, and already know what they need from others, could teach potential caregivers, nurses and teachers? Why not have disabled adults meet with the parents of disabled children to give them encouragement and hope as well as ideas for adaptations? Why not arrange for disabled teens to mentor disabled children? Why not invent a space where disabled adults could be consultants to schools and even the universities to create truly accessible learning environments? Why not build some accessible housing and provide wheelchair transportation to enable students to attend any one of the many colleges in Botswana? Why not find someone to teach disabled persons the business skills they need to create businesses, hire able-bodied workers, and thrive as creative entrepreneurs? Dr. Amanze had let loose a tiger, and I wasn't sure if I had it by the tail or not!

Andrew and Gladys had seen little children wandering around in the streets, neglected and sometimes abused because their mothers were sick with HIV/AIDS. Even when other family members were supposed to be caring for the little ones, they weren't always able to manage. When the Mudereri's realized the extent of the unmet need in their area, they prayed and did something about it. They didn't wait around for someone else to do it. They didn't excuse themselves from involvement because of their other responsibilities. They simply began with seven children that Andrew had found being mistreated. Without any money, any corporate or international sponsors, without even any encouragement from his church members, Andrew brought them to the church and Gladys began caring for them. All they had was a passion that God had put into their hearts – God's own passionate love for His children, all of them.

God has blessed their faith and their faithfulness. Today, eighty preschoolers are well-fed and energetically loved in a beautiful facility where certified teachers help them learn. Many individuals, churches and businesses have joined forces to help support their work in various ways. Those kids will be ready to enter primary school when they graduate, as others have before them. Many of these children will also return to the Day Care Centre in the afternoons to join the approximately thirty other children who come daily after school for lunch, for help with homework, and for supervised games. Children who once had no future have a bright one now because two ordinary Christians trusted God and proved it by opening their doors. Trust and obey. There's that phrase again.

Maleboga went home to Serowe not long after I returned to the U.S., but she remains in my heart and in my prayers. So do the inescapable questions sparked by the challenge posed by God to Christians, a challenge to love God's children, exemplified in the Mudereri's life and expressed by Dr. Amanze.

Lead me, Lord. Lead me in Thy righteousness. Make Thy way plain before my face. And make me willing to keep on following when you do!

CHAPTER TWENTY-SEVEN

Great Is Thy Faithfulness

Coming back to the States turned out to be almost unbearably difficult. I had actually felt more at home in Africa than I had ever felt anywhere before, and I didn't want to leave then, or ever! I hadn't learned enough yet to be really useful, and so much that I wanted to accomplish remained unfinished; so many possibilities had to be left unexplored. My school assignments had all been emailed and the evaluations typed.

My six months abroad never actually seemed like a completed graduation requirement. It felt like my life. All I could think about was returning to Botswana, to the people who were dear to me, the language I loved, and the culture that embraced me.

In Botswana, God had shown me His faithfulness over and over in both remarkable and quite ordinary ways. I was never alone and partner-less after all; instead, God had given me many partners – African, English and American. And far from being a limitation, my disability (as Dr. Frost had predicted) turned out to be my greatest advantage, a kind of automatic door opener.

Although I was happy to see my family and friends, and to use my electric wheelchair again, I found myself for the first time in my life, homesick. I missed the cheerful taxi drivers and the energetic Day Care Centre children. I missed my African family, my friends, and the sounds and smells of Botswana. Mostly, I missed myself. I felt like a stranger in a strange land.

It was my grandpa who urged me to be content as I began my senior year at SBU, and to use that time wisely. He was shy, and for him to

Me as "Tidbit"

speak openly about God was extremely rare. But one hot July afternoon, Grandpa gently insisted that I choose to be content, to settle back into my life as a student and continue to prepare myself, so that I would be ready to do whatever God asked of me in the future. He knew, even if I did not, that every goal I might reach pointed directly to the next one, and my past preparation was insufficient for that future, whatever it would turn out to be.

That was the last long, solemn conversation we ever had. A few weeks later, he had the first of several small strokes that slowed his speech and clouded his memory. My grandpa, who had helped me through so many hard times, had tutored me and entertained me with stories, seemed to fade right before my eyes. It was a terrible and unexpected grief, but I am so grateful for that last, long discussion, and glad he had lived to welcome me back from Botswana and into his warm embrace. He loved me. He had confidence in me.

So I turned my attention again toward school. I still met my Botswana friends on Facebook and in email, but I tried to keep my heart quiet and focused on the work I still had to do here. With ICS classes complete, my senior year consisted mostly of meeting requirements for my second major, Speech Communications/Theatre. Even though I obviously couldn't physically construct a set, it was wonderful fun to try to design one, and to learn the terminology and techniques of stagecraft. Hopefully, someday I could teach it to someone with hands, someone who might work with disabled actors in Botswana or elsewhere. But my favorite class that fall turned out to be Directing Plays. Before going abroad I never would have had the confidence to do this work – to take up both the responsibility and the privilege of directing other people's performance so that a story might be well-told. But Africa had changed me. Now I was ready.

To be a servant of any art requires integrity, risk-taking and compassion. Emily had told me that years before when I began to draw, and now I discovered it again in a different artistic form. Directing forced me to discover how best to serve the actors in a theatre production so they could serve the story. It was the opposite of what we tend to think of as "leadership." The only authority I had was my own study, research and conviction about the story itself, its purpose, and its power. My heavy responsibility was to open that vision to the performers, and then to trust them to reveal it in their performance. Difficult? Absolutely. But it satisfied me deeply and changed the way I will approach any leadership responsibility in the future.

Each class I took offered me new perspectives and insights, not just directly by giving me information I hadn't had before, but by interacting (at least in my mind) with every other class I'd had. My SBU education seemed to work that way from the beginning. That last year I came to recognize that no course actually ever ended for me, because what I'd learned in one class kept emerging again later to influence how I heard something else. I have never yet escaped the questions posed in my very first class, Spiritual Formation – "What's the bottom line? How's that working for you?" Pauline Epistles affected how I understood the ethics of Economics and challenged some of what I read for that class. What I learned in Cultural and Global Awareness shed light on some of our current immigration debates. African History and Politics affected what I remembered of my Ethnography and Strategy class. Directing Plays served as a reflection on what I'd begun to discover in my Apprenticeship Practicum in Botswana, and Barefoot Language

Learning made its way into Cross-Cultural Communication. Everything, even Biology, Algebra and Computers, began to sing together to create in me one single hymn of gratitude. I had finally, it seemed, come to have eyes to see what education was really all about. It was beautiful. It was God's.

So when the audition announcement for Something To Do With William Shakespeare appeared on the bulletin board, my name was one of the first to be scribbled in. I had said I was going to audition someday, and here was my opportunity. There wasn't any guarantee that I'd get a part. Thankfully, it doesn't work that way. Nobody was catering to me, and I didn't want anyone to cater to me. But I did want a chance to try. Dr. Sartwell gave me that opportunity. She wrote, "When Minda first asked me if I would ever permit someone in a wheelchair to audition for a play at SBU, I was a little taken aback. Theatre has long been open to disabled performers and audiences, and the thought never occurred to me that a person wouldn't be able to participate in a play because of a physical disability. As long as a person has talent, drive, and a willingness to create, that person can be a vital part of a production. Period."

Still, the day after those fall auditions, when my name showed up beside the character "Tidbit," I almost couldn't breathe for sheer excitement! Our comedy, created by using monologues lifted from various Shakespearean plays, grew and evolved over several weeks. Everyone participated in that process, in which ridiculous suggestions were actually taken seriously, and sometimes accepted. With some first-rate actors (of which I am not!), the production was hilarious. It was an immense privilege to sit in the company of those students and faculty, and watch how story-telling works when really creative actors and actresses do it well. I ate, breathed and dreamed theatre that fall as I memorized lines and worked to use both my body and my voice to give my character, well, character!

There were a few people who worried about how much the theatre production might have to be adapted to accommodate my disability. These were essentially the same questions that had been asked about my very presence at SBU, and again before my six months abroad. I

156

felt less anxious this time, though, because I knew what Dr. Sartwell thought about it all. Dr. Sartwell wrote, "It bothered me to hear people say that we had to make 'accommodations' in order for Minda to be onstage. To say that we had to 'accommodate' her implies that we had to 'settle' for a product that was somehow less than (or at least other than) our 'ideal' production. Of course we faced challenges as a result of Minda's disabilities, but neither Mr. Wehmeyer nor I shy away from challenges. Any good theatre artist knows that obstacles and difficulties make for a much stronger production because they force directors, actors, and designers to re-think assumptions. Logistically speaking, we had to deal with some things that we hadn't encountered before. For example, we had to create a costume that would fit Minda and allow her to move easily on the stage. Obviously, there is no pattern for such a costume! We worked by trial and error to accomplish her final look – which was adorable, by the way, as effective as every other costume in the show. It was another challenge to make it possible for Minda to move from one place to another backstage. It can be difficult for an able-bodied actor to exit from one side of the stage and then enter from another. For Minda, this was even more problematic. The floor was dirty, sometimes cluttered, and she had to move fast. So we relied on a crew member to wheel her from one side of the stage to another between scenes. But it worked. Any production (at SBU anyway) is a collaborative creation of the actors, directors, and designers. Since Minda was a part of the production process from the ground up, we just created a way of telling the story that worked for her and for everybody else in the production."

I discovered something, too. Having lived without my electric wheelchair for six months, I found it much more natural to be on the floor a lot, even around adults, and to move easily and quickly across a room. I hadn't done much of that since I was a little girl, and it felt terrific to be free of the chair. This made it easier than Dr. Sartwell had probably expected when directing me in this play.

Dr. Sartwell wrote, "One challenge I had faced with Minda in her earlier acting classes involved her wheelchair. When she performed in it, her performances were sometimes stiff. She had no room to move.

157

But once she abandoned the security of her chair, she transformed into the most animated performer in the class. She consistently scored higher on physical expression than did her classmates who have arms and legs. Minda has the most expressive way of moving her shoulders. She doesn't have an arm, but she can point just like anybody else. She doesn't have legs, but she quickly developed multiple "walking" styles. She could amble, she could hop, she could stomp. It was a joy to watch Minda embrace what her body could do for her as a storyteller."

In this performance, I actually did have to stomp my foot in anger, jump up as if to claw at the eyes of my much taller rival, and finally, to chase her up some low stairs, all the while menacing her with my voice and facial expressions. "Tidbit" was tiny, but she was also shockingly aggressive. It cracked people up to see the visual contrast between us, partly because it was clear to everybody that I didn't feel any embarrassment about using my body to surprise the audience into laughter. I didn't realize that hardly anyone on campus had ever seen me out of my wheelchair, so it didn't occur to me that it would totally stun them to see me hurl myself up some steps in angry pursuit. Those performances were sheer play, playful, and difficult all at the same time!

My grandpa died early one morning in late November. It felt as if the sun had gone out. Christmas came quietly that year. Grief numbed my heart and made it hard to sing or to join in the festivities. My mom obviously shared that sorrow, so we spent a lot of time together doing little but drinking Earl Grey tea, telling stories and reminding each other what a privilege it had been to have him for nearly 95 years. He had looked forward to seeing me graduate, and I felt that particular loss acutely.

Tears came less often by the time my final semester began, although there were still moments when I wanted more than anything to tell him, and only him, something I'd learned or an idea I'd had. The pain is easier now, but there is really no way to get closure, and I wouldn't want it if there were. Death is an enemy. God knows that. The fear of death and the power of death is part of what He came to conquer. In Him, there is only life and peace. But in us, separated from those we love, the ache is real. Scripture never tells us not to grieve. Paul's concern is that we not grieve like those who have no hope. Someday death will be swallowed up in victory forever, and all of those we have loved and lost will be returned to us whole, redeemed, glorious in Christ, as we ourselves will also be. I do not see it. But I believe it.

With graduation just around the corner, my spring classes demanded attention. There were speeches to compose and deliver and long papers I needed to write. But during all the busyness, my heart kept rejoicing in all that God had done for me through all my life. Words weren't adequate, so I sang, mostly under my breath.

"Great is Thy faithfulness, O God, my Father, there is no shadow of turning with Thee…" There has been plenty of "turning" with me, but not with You.

"…Thy compassions they fail not…" No, but mine failed, over and over.

"Morning by morning new mercies I see." Seen and rejoiced to see. And how many more have I not even noticed?

"All I have needed, thy hand hath provided…" Oh, Lord, more than I have needed. Far more.

"Great is thy faithfulness, Lord unto me." Yes, and yes, and yes— to me, and to all who call upon you. That is the reality of our ordinary Christian experience, and its bottom line—God is faithful.

CHAPTER TWENTY-EIGHT

I Want to Walk as a Child of the Light

It didn't seem possible. In less than five hours I was going to drive my wheelchair across that broad cement walkway in front of Mabee Chapel and receive my degree along with so many of my friends. It had been raining for days, but this one dawned clear. I could hear my mom and Grandmother Marian in the kitchen making breakfast, but I stayed in bed a few minute longer, musing. How did I ever manage to make it to this day? You alone, O Lord, are my strength, my song. But so many times I almost quit. Your faithfulness kept me faithful. I couldn't have done it without so many others. We are one in the bond of love.

I should have been nervous, but I wasn't. A few weeks earlier, I learned that I had been chosen to deliver the Senior Speech. I wanted what I wrote to speak for all who were graduating. For days I'd worked on it to make sure the words I would say to the crowd of families and friends would reflect all that was in my heart. I had rehearsed it late into the night, but now I felt ready.

My black gown hung on the closet door frame, pressed. A member of St. Alban's had carefully hemmed it up and shortened the sleeves to accommodate my arms. A friend arrived to style my hair, recently cut and highlighted for the day. I must have eaten breakfast, but I don't remember it. I do remember my mom and her ever-present camera taking too many photos, and Marian sitting across the room, quiet and smiling.

160

I walked over to the school early, by myself, an ordinary senior going onto campus for the last time of my university career, to stand beside students and teachers whose lives had changed mine forever. Dr. Frost met with the ICS seniors once we were ready in our caps and gowns, laughed and posed for photos. Then he prayed for us, and thanked God for all we had learned, for all we had been given, for all we would do. Soon we merged with all the other graduates, and the bagpipe player began playing as purple ribbons waved from the front of the Chapel. The atmosphere was electric. Slowly, we followed our teachers onto the mall and made our way, two by two, to the area reserved for us. Suddenly the enormity of this day overwhelmed me, and I had to blink back tears.

The program began, and when the time came, I carefully wheeled myself up the ramp that had been constructed for me, put the binder on a music stand, grinned at the student who helped me keep the pages from blowing in the wind, and began to speak.

"Dr. Taylor, Dr. Brown, members of the Board of Trustees, faculty and staff of SBU, families and friends, I am honored to be speaking on behalf of all of us who are graduating today. My life story is not very different from all of the stories that my friends here could tell you about their lives. Each of us is unique, of course. Each life is. But together they represent only different experiences of the ONE, great, God-story—the story of His redemption and His call.

My story is just one example of a life that has been shaped and directed because of spending a few years in this place, surrounded by people who love God and who have loved us with His love. It is not sentimental to say that. It is simply the truth.

Throughout my life, long before I heard of SBU, God was good to me. He has always done more than I could ask or even dare to imagine. Because I was born with an inconvenient disability, there were many simple things I could not do as a child. But as I was growing up in my adoptive family, I was surrounded by believers. Each of them helped me to discover that I had choices. I could give my life to the Lord, and allow Him to use me for his glory – OR I could suffer the frustration of my disability for no purpose at all. I could believe

161

With mom at St. Alban's Episcopal Church

that to those who love God, all things work together for good, or I could choose to be angry with God, the world, my disability, and myself. I chose God. But it was not always easy. Not for me, and not for any of the rest of us whose struggles have been different, but just as real.

When I began to study the Bible, to struggle with mathematics, to immerse myself in missions' courses and theatre rehearsals, I found that despite my anxiety, God met me every time and gave me freedom and peace, and decent grades besides! When I wore myself out writing papers, working late studying for exams, and drinking too much coffee just to stay awake, I realized I was not so much disabled, but ordinary, just like all my friends who were doing the same things.

When the Redford faculty sent me out on my six months abroad in Africa despite my handicap, and when the theatre faculty put me up on stage despite the difficulty of adapting the costume and the stage blocking to accommodate my legless self, I realized that I was just an ordinary young SBU woman being mentored and encouraged and prodded to achieve – just exactly like everybody else. For me, those were gifts that I can never repay, but for which I am grateful.

During these years, even when most of us didn't recognize it at all, God has been working through everything we have encountered here—the good, the bad, and the astonishing, in order to prepare each of us for the future we still do not see clearly. But sometimes God gives us a glimpse of how beautiful that future can be as we live in the power of His love. I have discovered, as many of us have found, that living confidently by the Spirit of God right here and right now allows us to pledge allegiance to Christ's new Kingdom that is still coming, but that is also already visible. So I am content to live a risen life with Christ now, even before the End comes and we are all happy with the Lord forever.

We know that we have been crucified with Christ and raised to new life in Him, and given freedom and joy, and a good SBU education—FOR A REASON. None of us see all the reasons yet. But we see some of them: We know our life counts; we know that what we do with it matters; we know that we are responsible for what we have learned, to use our knowledge wisely and well; we know that God has the right to ask anything of us; we know a little of the cost of discipleship; and we know that God can be trusted. Pray for us that we will walk worthy of these gifts and offer them freely to others in service of Jesus Christ.

On behalf of each of us who are graduating today, I want, first, to thank our families and friends for making it possible for us to come, and to remain, at SBU. Your encouragement meant more than you probably suspect. And I also want to thank the faculty who prayed for us, and sometimes with us; the teachers who came to class even when they were tired or discouraged, but came with a grin, or a song; the professors who made sense of algebraic formulas, and those who assigned long papers and then actually read every word. I want to thank the women and men who kept the buildings clean, and the library open; the ones who cooked our meals, and the ones who shoveled the walks so my wheelchair could get across campus in February – and May!

I also need to thank the class of 2013 for showing me what Christian community looks like. I would not be graduating without the help of my friends. Many of you have opened doors for me, carried my backpack, helped get out my pens and paper and heavy books. You've carried trays full of food, walked with me in the pouring rain, made sure I didn't slip on the ice, and cheered me on when I was ready to give up. I will never forget that.

I love both my majors, and I know God will use them as I serve him cross-culturally, but I might never have heard my calling at all if I had not come to SBU. It is at my University that I found my vocation, my vision, and my voice. My calling is missions. Other graduates will follow Jesus as accountants or teachers or sociologists, businessmen or pastors, actors, musicians or scientists. But all of us who are graduating today are looking forward. We have learned about discipleship, what it will cost us to exercise our gifts with integrity and with gladness, because of the grace of an SBU education. We feel ready to walk into our future. And we are grateful. Thank you."

I had not been able to get through it without tears. I meant every word I said. As I started to leave the platform, Dr. Brown turned me around to face the whole audience on their feet, clapping and cheering. That sight broke my composure, and yet it also filled me with astonished joy.

I had only been in my place for a few minutes when Dr. Taylor stood to announce the names of the two students who would receive the Life Beautiful Award. Until this moment, the faculty selections had been kept a tightly guarded secret. I craned my neck to hear, hoping that my friend Sarah had been chosen, or if not Sarah, then our friend Amber. When he called my name I was so flustered that I didn't know what to do. Shocked, I didn't move. "It's you. Go on up there," someone prodded. Never did I expect this.

True, my life was beautiful. It had been made beautiful. But that beauty had all been given to me, none of it was mine. How could SBU honor me for that? All I can guess is that the faculty had decided to honor God, to simply give Him praise for what He had used them to do in me and for me.

I came to those men and women as an insecure, anxious, defensive and stubborn young woman, afraid of taking classes outside my comfort zone, hungry to serve God but unwilling to even pursue a degree until I was practically forced to do it. That was my gift to the faculty.

What they gave to me in return was their patience, their wealth of knowledge, and their own Christ-inspired strength under pressure. They modeled prayer for me, as well as hope, joy, and the beauty of a life lived in service to Christ Jesus, the Lord. That was their gift to me. If I go on to live a life worthy of that honor, and I pray that I will, it will be because of SBU.

Three times that morning I rolled up the ramp, finally receiving that purple cardboard roll, evidence that I had, indeed, met all the requirements for graduation. By that time, all my earlier tears had gone, replaced by laughter, right out loud! From now on, any time anyone asks me to give my testimony, I will think of that day.

Soon after graduation, my African parents, Andrew and Gladys

Mudereri, came to visit me and to see SBU. For three weeks we talked and dreamed about what needs to be done in Botswana to help other disabled Christians take their place in society, and increasingly, to serve Jesus Christ in the churches. I hope to return soon to my African home. But no matter what happens, no matter where I end up, I have finally allowed God to carve one little phrase deeply into my heart—trust and obey.

Kathleen Thomerson, a 20th century Episcopal hymn writer composed this song. I sing it a lot, because it is the truth.

> I want to walk as a child of the Light. I want to follow Jesus.
> God set the stars to give light to the world.
> The star of my life is Jesus.
> In Him there is no darkness at all.
> The night and the day are both alike.
> The Lamb is the light of the city of God
> Shine in my heart, Lord Jesus.
> I want to see the brightness of God. I want to look at Jesus.
> Clear sun of righteousness, shine on my path,
> and show me the way to the Father.
> I'm looking for the coming of Christ. I want to be with Jesus.
> When we have run with patience the race,
> we shall know the joy of Jesus.

The most ordinary, broken lives can shine with the beauty of God's glory, when we allow it. And when we do, it is obvious to everyone that it is God's glory, not our own.

Amen. Come, Lord Jesus!

"Diginity"

167

"Perseverance"

168

"October"

169

If you would like to contact Minda or purchase prints of her artwork, please visit her website: www.mindacox.com or e-mail: minda204@aol.com

About Minda Cox Art

Art has always been my passion, although it has only been within the last few years that I have had a teacher who believed I could paint despite my disability. I love watercolor, because I enjoy the sense of movement, and the freedom of the water and color working together to produce even more than I had first envisioned. I love even the uncertainty about exactly how an idea will turn out once the paint touches the wet paper. It appeals to the side of me that wants to fly, to take risks. When I discovered that I could use pen and watercolor together I

Minda Cox

began to develop a new combination of gesture drawings and paint on vellum. This is fun for me and is another way for me to express my freedom. I also love pencil, because I can work slowly and carefully and make changes if I want to. It is restful, which appeals to another, quieter part of me.

Everything I want to do and cannot do with my body, art does for me and in me. My art dances when I cannot; my paint runs for me when I am bound to my wheelchair. The colors jump and clap for joy, although I cannot do either of those things apart from my art. I do not paint dark things because my life is not sad, but the absence of arms and legs does involve real physical limitations that art somehow diminishes. I hope the viewer will sense that freedom in my work.

My driving force is God: God who created me with the capacity to be creative. Discovery of the gift of art in myself gives me joy, and confidence that God has made me in his image, and is calling me to use my gifts of art and speaking to give delight, and to express beauty.

I hope also to encourage women in some third world or other impoverished area to demonstrate by the creative and colorful works of their hands that the joy of Jesus shines even where despair ought to reign, and also to discover that their artistic skills can help them provide for their families. ∎